Other Books by Theo Prodromitis
The Success Formula
Big Questions During Tough Times: A Journey to Rediscover Yourself

THE BALANCE BETWEEN HUSTLE & FLOW

KNOWING WHEN TO MAKE THINGS HAPPEN AND WHEN TO LET THEM HAPPEN

THEO PRODROMITIS

BALBOA.PRESS
A DIVISION OF HAY HOUSE

Copyright © 2020 Theo Prodromitis.

All rights reserved. No part of this book may be used or reproduced by any means, graphic, electronic, or mechanical, including photocopying, recording, taping or by any information storage retrieval system without the written permission of the author except in the case of brief quotations embodied in critical articles and reviews.

Balboa Press books may be ordered through booksellers or by contacting:

Balboa Press
A Division of Hay House
1663 Liberty Drive
Bloomington, IN 47403
www.balboapress.com
844-682-1282

Because of the dynamic nature of the Internet, any web addresses or links contained in this book may have changed since publication and may no longer be valid. The views expressed in this work are solely those of the author and do not necessarily reflect the views of the publisher, and the publisher hereby disclaims any responsibility for them.

The author of this book does not dispense medical advice or prescribe the use of any technique as a form of treatment for physical, emotional, or medical problems without the advice of a physician, either directly or indirectly. The intent of the author is only to offer information of a general nature to help you in your quest for emotional and spiritual well-being. In the event you use any of the information in this book for yourself, which is your constitutional right, the author and the publisher assume no responsibility for your actions.

Any people depicted in stock imagery provided by Getty Images are models, and such images are being used for illustrative purposes only.
Certain stock imagery © Getty Images.

Print information available on the last page.

ISBN: 978-1-9822-5365-3 (sc)
ISBN: 978-1-9822-5364-6 (hc)
ISBN: 978-1-9822-5366-0 (e)

Library of Congress Control Number: 2020916465

Balboa Press rev. date: 09/16/2020

CONTENTS

Acknowledgments vii
Introduction ix

Part I　　　The World of All Possibilities 1

Chapter 1　Light Your Fire 3
Chapter 2　Western Hustle Meets Eastern Flow: How Wayne Dyer
　　　　　　Changed My Life 12

Part II　　　A Look Within 27

Chapter 3　The First Influence: Family & Early Beginnings 29
Chapter 4　The Second Influence: Your Interpersonal Environment:
　　　　　　Relationships 36
Chapter 5　The Third Influence: Mindset 44
Chapter 6　The Fourth Influence: Choices 55
Chapter 7　The Fifth Influence: Passion 69
Chapter 8　The Sixth Influence: Serendipity 77

Part III　　The Big Questions 85

Chapter 9　　The First Question: What Do I Really Want? 87
Chapter 10　The Second Question: Who Can I Serve? 96
Chapter 11　The Third Question: How Will I Adopt this New
　　　　　　　Awareness? 106

References 119
Video Resources 123
Additional Resources: Books 125
About the Author 127

ACKNOWLEDGMENTS

I would first like to acknowledge the contribution of my editor and friend Jess Larsen Brennan, your divine presence in my life helped organize and bring every word to life. You helped convince me that my story deserved to be told. To Laura Schaefer, I give my gratitude for bringing me through the rigors of refining and developing my writing. I extend my greatest appreciation for my Director of Business Development, Lauriane Cardot, whose energy and excellence brings out the best in me. I am forever thankful to all of you. We did it!

I would also like to thank every single one of my teachers (and I mean adversaries too) that have come into my life to help me stretch, grow and seek deeper meaning in serving others. If you are reading this, you know who you are.

Thank you to my family, for which I am inextricably connected. I am a whisper of my Greek ancestors, grandmother's prayers, and grandfather's hard work. The unconditional love and inspiration of my magical parents Mary and Spero Prodromitis is in every cell of my being. My sister Themie is the most unbelievable sister I could ever ask for, kind and nurturing and relentlessly loyal. Your achievements and compassion are unrivaled. Dean is my brother, my friend, business partner and role model. You are the kindest badass I know. Themie and Dean are my strength and love, thank you for grounding me.

Humbly, I thank my children Mary, Jacqueline and Spero. You give my life meaning and purpose and unlimited, unbridled curiosity and love. You are my reason for everything and my inspiration for this book. I dedicate it to Mary, Jacqueline and Spero and pray you feel the unfathomable depth of my love for you on every page.

I can do all things through Christ who strengthens me. -Phillipians 4:13

INTRODUCTION

I was recently invited to the opportunity of a lifetime: a retreat on "Compassionate Leadership" in Dharamshala, where His Holiness the 14th Dalai Lama resides in exile from Tibet. It culminated with private teachings with the Dalai Lama himself. Wow. I could only attribute the invitation to the grace of the good Lord, hard work, and my divine calling to grow spiritually, learn more, and share it with the world. My plan was to complete the final chapter of this very book, *The Balance Between Hustle and Flow* in this sacred town, at the foothills of the Himalayas in India.

When I was first invited, I said yes immediately without even looking at cost or distance. The Dalai Lama? Compassionate Leadership retreat? Collaborating with twenty amazing colleagues from around the world as part of the Zuckerberg Institute?

Yes, yes, and *yes*.

I jumped on Google to see that the destination was 8,000 miles away and would require four separate flights—Tampa to NYC, NYC to Dubai, Dubai to Delhi, and Delhi to Dharamshala. India is nine and a half hours ahead of EST.

In essence, it is already tomorrow there.

The region of McLeod Ganj is at an elevation of 6,831 feet. I vacation in Denver (elevation 5,000 ft.) and Breckenridge (elevation 12,000 ft) in the summer, so I figured I could handle the foothills of the Himalayas. If Brad Pitt could make *Seven Years in Tibet* near there, I knew in my heart: "I've got this."

In the months of preparation for my first trip to Asia, I learned so much about what we take for granted in the United States. The visa application process with the Indian government was intense. They asked multiple questions about my heritage, parents, and Pakistan. They wanted to know if I had ever been charged with or convicted of anything. They needed to know who I was, where I had been, why I was coming to the country, how long I planned to stay…and more. It was standard to be asked all these questions because I was seeking to enter their country.

Next, I needed to visit my doctor to find out what vaccinations were required. Here in the States, we take for granted the lack of diseases and health risks (more on this topic in a moment). Many of the vaccines were "optional," but who wants to travel to an area with active cholera, malaria, Japanese encephalitis, yellow fever, Hepatitis A & B, diphtheria, and pertussis without full protection? Not me. Our organizer recommended bringing a full supply of over-the-counter medications as well, just in case…Imodium, Benadryl, Advil, TUMS, Dramamine. It made me so grateful for our ready access to healthcare. (While our system is far from perfect, we do have access and far fewer diseases to contend with on a daily basis than other places around the globe.)

The air quality in New Delhi reached hazardous levels the week of my planned departure. Per an article in *Time* magazine, "On Nov. 3, the level of PM 2.5 was more than 23 times higher than the corresponding WHO air quality guidelines, according to data from the Indian Central Pollution Control Board." Although I would only be passing through there to my final destination, the warning I read said, "Many planes are grounded, some pilots are trained to fly in the dense fog … but some are not."

I realized that in my daily life, I even take air quality for granted.

Immediately prior to departure, my 15-year-old daughter Jacqueline came into my room and started chatting. I had so many details racing through my brain that I said, "I am so stressed out!"

Calmly and firmly, she responded, "I understand. Everyone gets stressed out. But what is important is what you do with it. You can let it get to you or decide to power through it or leave it aside."

Wise words, as it turned out.

Our teachers are everywhere.

I went into this adventure thinking that the big lessons would come from His Holiness the Dalai Lama and his teachers in the sacred place of Dharamshala through meditation, yoga, and mindfulness teaching at the Compassionate Leadership retreat. But when I landed in New York and went to the Emirates counter to check in for the international flight from NY to Dubai, everything shifted in a moment.

Destiny had different plans than I did.

I was about to get a big lesson in when to hustle…and when to go with the flow.

You're Not Going Anywhere

When I handed the agent my travel visa, she frowned and said, "I am sorry. I cannot accept this."

My heart sank. My mind raced. My ego roared. Welcome to uncertainty—the birthplace of the battle between hustle and flow. I had a choice to make: how hard to push.

We went over the issue, and she got her supervisor… who concurred there was nothing he could do. My visa was rejected because some of my documents listed my prior married name and some listed my maiden name.

After months of preparation, going over every detail, the completely unexpected had happened. Here was my chance to step up and handle one of those things with grace. So, I remembered my 17-year-old daughter Mary saying, "If anything happens, Mommy, just book a hotel room in the city and enjoy writing while you are there."

She knows I thrive on the energy of New York and my creativity peaks when I feel at home. Wise words. Kind heart, she knows me so well.

I met three wonderful people in the city during that time of uncertainty who all supported my journey. The Uber driver who picked me up after I learned I could not board the plane was from India (of course) and he listened to the emotionally charged rendition of my plight. He shared that he came here from India and his family was still there; he loved New York and they loved India. I cannot explain how important it was for me to have such a wonderful, driven, bright person there while I was dealing with the possibility of not reaching India or meeting the Dalai Lama at all. Holding space for a stranger is a superpower and you may never know the ripples of goodness that it will bring when you offer it.

My second teacher was a server at John's Pizza on 44th Street, near my hotel. She somehow made time (in a bustling Times Square restaurant) to listen to my situation and shared how she came over from Albania when she was young. Her warmth, kindness, and caring reminded me that grace and compassion come in all forms.

She carried a maternal strength—you know, the kind you need when you are unsure of the outcome of something. It was like an old friend telling me that it was going to all work out for the best.

I spent all day Friday at the Indian Consulate. Eight long hours of filling out forms, waiting, getting photocopies, money orders, phone calls to high-ranking government officials, and more. At 3 p.m., it was *finally* confirmed that they could/would not help me.

"What?! WT_! WT_! You are kidding me, right?!" was all I could think.

I really needed to remember my own advice. I was being put to the test. Every sentence they said to me began with, "You should have," "You could have," "You must…"

It all started to sound the same, like the low murmur of muttered nonsense we used in theater class when we were on stage pretending to carry on conversations in the background: "peas and carrots, peas and carrots, rhubarb, rhubarb."

In the end, the message was clear:

You are not going anywhere.

It ended with them telling me to fly to Atlanta. (*Are you kidding me? It was Friday at almost 5 p.m.*) My private audience with His Holiness the Dalai Lama was just days away! I prayed for the grace to be calm and kind and listen to the signs and the universe.

I checked back into the hotel in disbelief, somewhat defeated. The bellman, Jaime, saw that I had checked out earlier and was checking back in, so he asked if everything was okay. Here was another teacher/stranger leading the way with compassion when he could have easily been too busy to even notice me. We chatted on the way up to a beautiful room with a view of the magnificent lights of Broadway. He was kind and a great listener. I felt better after telling him what had happened. He genuinely cared (held space), and that made a huge difference in my life.

One More Teacher

The next day, I boarded a plane back home to Tampa, absolutely ecstatic at the reality of going home to my children (even if the plan was to fly back out to India on Monday).

The plane was packed as always, yet I actually had an empty seat next to me and was thrilled about it—finally, another chance to write! But then, a man about 6' 4" came quickly down the aisle. Of course, he was sitting directly next to me. He may have sensed my disappointment (or perhaps I have no poker face), and he said, "Hi, I know you wish I was not here."

Oh no, did I feel bad. I sincerely replied, "Not at all, I am happy you made it on the plane; everyone is on a journey of their own."

He was so relieved and we got ready for takeoff. New York to Tampa is not a very long flight, so I resigned myself to the fact that I couldn't break out my laptop and write with him next to me. I needed to just relax or read or write long-hand in my planner. We exchanged names and immediately found a common bond. His name was Nigel Ashley and his family called him Ashley because many family members were also called Nigel.

His whole life in the United States, he has been mistaken for a woman. My name is Theo and my whole life, I have been mistaken for a man. My name always raises an eyebrow when we both meet someone. They can't help but say, "Isn't Ashley a girl's name? Isn't Theo a man's name?"

We went on to have the most delightful spiritual chat. It turned out he had been to India for a yoga retreat with his wife. We love many of the same authors and share a common outlook and love of Dr. Wayne Dyer and his work. Time flew by and we became friends in that short period of time. Ashley was clearly another teacher sent directly in my path.

It felt like serendipity.

You should know that I pride myself on being a driven, creative, optimistic, and solution-oriented person. Many times, I hear myself giving advice to someone down on their luck that goes a little something like this....

"Listen to the signs."

"Don't force things."

"It will work out for the best."

"God's delays are not God's denials."

And of course, the biggest one…

"Everything happens for a reason."

At every step of my non-journey to India, I needed to be kind and compassionate toward myself and toward each and every person who told me no. "Everything happens for a reason" worked perfectly fine while I still believed that my trip would work out. "Listening to the signs" resonated when I thought I would still get the outcome *I* wanted. "It will work out for the best" meant I would be upgraded to First Class and meet the man of my dreams…right?

Well.

The problem was, I was *attached* to all of it. And I was learning that the advice I routinely gave to others was harder to accept when nothing was working out for me. I was attached to my plan, to its timing, to being right, to going, to what I imagined I would learn.

So, when my new visa arrived via email Monday morning (as a result of my relentless Friday night happy hour efforts at the Marriott Marquis after being rebuked at the embassy), I phoned the airline, fully believing I was still going, I was shocked to hear it would cost $7,000 to change my ticket. They checked every route out of every American city and the best they could do was $7,000.

Sigh.

A prayer.

Grace. Maybe everything *was* working out just fine. I was not going anywhere and it was okay. It wasn't my time to meet His Holiness the Dalai Lama or to travel to India. Nevertheless, my journey was complete, and my lessons were well-learned.

I looked in temples, churches, and mosques. But I found the Divine within my heart.

Preparation for the Ever-Shifting Now

The story of not meeting the Dalai Lama happened in November of 2019. It was profound and somehow prepared me for what was going to happen to the world in early 2020. COVID-19 (Coronavirus) showed up in China first in December 2019 and then spread to the entire world… deadly, contagious, and rampant. By March 2020, entire countries were on quarantine and businesses shut down. The uncertainty was chilling and the world turned upside down. Just months before the pandemic began, when I was to go on my spiritual journey, the US economy was booming, with the Dow reaching 28,000 and record low unemployment in all sectors.

COVID-19 brought the world to its knees. It was the great equalizer because the virus did not discriminate on grounds of country, ethnicity, income, or gender. Unfortunately, however, it hit the elderly and people with compromised immune systems hardest. The lack of complete data on how many people contracted it with little to no symptoms made the true percentage of fatalities virtually impossible to calculate. Like no other pandemic, its origins were shrouded in mystery. Foreboding but true. This made it elusive and almost impossible to combat immediately.

Trials for a vaccine were in the works but at best would take a year. The race to find treatments was on. The balance between hustle and flow had never been so relevant before in my lifetime. Everyone was petrified, yet many of us also realized the gift of being homebound. We hustled to follow the new directive of "social distancing" (staying six feet away from one another to avoid infection) and flowed in digging deep in our faith and family connections. It was a time to evaluate what was most necessary and important in our lives. As all world crises (the likes of which only wars could compare in my estimation), it gave birth to latent talent and innovation.

There was also, of course, the worst kinds of behavior on display, with some hoarding toilet paper (yes, toilet paper), hand sanitizer, surgical masks, and more. Grocery store shelves were bare and managers had to limit the number of shoppers in the store at once in order to create a safe environment. Those people who took part in political posturing or price gouging had a great deal to atone for. For the sake of this book about hustle and flow, suffice it to say they turned "hustle" into *abuse*. I remember a sad image of an elderly woman with a walker in a store with bare shelves. The caption read, "Think of her when you are hoarding more than you need." Overall, however, the triumph of goodness far outweighed the bad during the Coronavirus outbreak of 2020.

The flow of each immediate family unit being together could be described as a reckoning of sorts. In my neighborhood, my daughter Jacqueline and I went out to rake the leaves and noticed what seemed to be 50 new people jogging, biking, and walking through the neighborhood. Everyone was in groups of two or three and seemed to be calm and happy. More than anything else, it felt like flow. It wasn't the normal rushing vibe (or sounds of racing cars and garage doors opening for neighbors to rush inside) we had experienced there for the previous nine years we had lived in our house. While no one really stopped to chat due to social distancing, they looked up, smiled, and said hello.

Thus, a different world was born.

It only took a global pandemic to do it.

Thought leaders led with virtual summits, videos, and new connections. I was inspired by Jovan Glasgow to write *Big Questions for Tough Times, A Journey to Rediscover Yourself,* and did webinars to benefit the Working Women Foundation funding female businesses, Feeding America, Joyful Heart Foundation, 3 Wishes for Ruby's Residents and the ICU Nurses at NY Health in Harlem. My brother Dean purchased a pallet of hand sanitizer and donated to First Responders, Healthcare Heroes, and Essential Workers. At the most difficult times (and these were unprecedented), making a contribution was so soothing to the soul.

I had family meetings with my three amazing children (all teenagers), Spero, Mary, and Jacqueline. It was critical for me to have daily discussions with them about this changing world. Spero asked so many deep questions that I developed amazing respect (even deeper than before, if possible) for his curiosity. He was relentless in reflecting the daily hustle questions, such as: "When can we go back to school? When will the stores open?" He also had flow questions, such as: "Why did this happen? Are the smartest people in the world working on a solution? What are we doing tomorrow?"

Mary was 17 and still wanted to socialize with friends but had a Zen-like strength that reminded me of my amazing mom. She was in flow when it was time for quarantine. Painting beautiful new artwork was her outlet and she spent hours painting and enjoying music (singing, playing instruments, and listening). Jacqueline made me so proud when she dedicated hours and days to creating art to send to one of my favorite charities. She got up and relentlessly created and shared the beauty of her soul. The charity, Three Wishes for Ruby's Residents, supports nursing home residents nationwide. It was started by an 11-year-old, Ruby Kate, to help nursing home residents feel loved. As a parent, this international pandemic crisis was a tremendous gift. I got to see my amazing children lean into the art of balancing hustle and flow.

The Balance

Every person striving for growth, passion, success, and excellence in their life has moments where they question whether to *hustle* for better, faster results or sit back, reflect, and let life *flow* for them. It is the most frequent advice I am asked for in life.

Achieving balance between these two concepts—and between the Eastern and Western mindsets and approaches that so many of us want to tap into simultaneously—is the challenge and the joy of our lives. This book is about working toward that balance. I'm far from perfect, but I've learned many lessons the hard way, and I am honored to share my journey—my balance—with you. Are you ready?

You're ready.

May all the grace of hustle and flow be available to you exactly when you need it.

PART I

THE WORLD OF ALL POSSIBILITIES

CHAPTER 1

LIGHT YOUR FIRE

Put yourself where preparation and opportunity meet, then strike a match. OPA!
Theo Prodromitis

No matter what circumstances in your life have led you to this moment, passion and excellence are available to you. In my humble opinion, they are indelibly stamped into your humanity, a part of your birthright of being human! If you woke up today, you have a purpose... and it will become more and more apparent to you as you pursue passion and excellence.

It is my distinct pleasure and great fortune to meet hundreds of inspiring people each year: seeing, sensing, and feeling the incredible spark within each individual. I'm insatiably curious, with a never-ending desire to catch a glimpse of the truth and connect with what is *really* going on inside others. I'm extremely interested in the hidden potential within each individual I encounter.

Like a sixth sense of sorts, I contemplate the magnificence of experience and imperfection that comprises each perfectly imperfect person. I wonder:

How are you *really* doing?

What are you spending precious time on? Is it something you love and meaningful?

Do you follow your passion in honor of your purpose?

Culture, ethnicity, and family patterns have an enormous influence on individual connection, passion, and potential. According to researchers, "Social and economic status of an individual or group can be measured as a blend of wealth, income, occupation, and education. Other contributors to social and economic status include race, ethnicity, home ownership, family size, family types, and even types of foods purchased. The combination of social and economic status can reveal a group or individual's access to resources, privilege, power, and control in a society."[1] I do not profess to be an expert in empirical data or social science research; rather I am an empath and "listener" to human potential. It is in my capacity as an empath and a listener that I am here to help you soar.

When pressed, many intelligent people will confide they just don't think they *have* a particular passion. Not for horses, or saving the planet, sous-vide cooking or trends in social media marketing.

But the fact remains: they are *amazing* at what they do.

Is that enough? Does that *count* as a passion? And is vocational passion required in order to lead a successful, fulfilling life?

It's easy to be passionate about your work when you *know in your bones* you are following your calling. If you are among the lucky ones who have this kind of gift, we will explore the ways to enhance, manage, and honor that gift.

But what about those who don't feel they are following a calling?

Just as many people don't think of themselves as having a passion for work; more still would say that their work is just…work. Do any of these statements resonate with you?

"It's just a job."

"It pays the bills."

"It is what I have to do to support my family."

---

[1] https://www.bls.gov/spotlight/2018/race-economics-and-social-status/pdf/race-economics-and-social-status.pdf Accessed April, 2020.

Yes, real life may take you sideways. Personal and professional challenges determine, influence, and shape your path. This certainly has been true for me, and I'll share some of the experiences of my life that appeared to be completely random as they were occurring...yet turned out to be incredibly significant with the benefit of hindsight.

It is my belief that even if you're not sure what your passion or hidden potential might be, you have one. If you're great at something that's "just a job," and not sure about the bigger picture, you're closer than you think to a breakthrough. Just a simple yearning for excellence is enough to help you discover incredible gifts within.

***Excellence* is often a more attainable goal than passion.**

Cultivating excellence in *whatever happens to be in front of you*—whether it's a job, a pursuit, a family obligation, or service to a cause—is much harder than talking about your potential. Striving for excellence is itself an act born of passion, and it requires commitment, faith, and perseverance.

It requires that you cultivate a deep inner "knowing" that there is more available than the status quo, that a higher standard is possible, that a vision only you can see will unfold.

There's a particular connection between passion and excellence that could teach us something about leading a meaningful, fulfilled life. There is an ember of potential and a point of light in every step of those who choose to walk in excellence and continuously take action, doing the next right thing without necessarily knowing where the path will lead. The most enduring stories of the ages reveal the means of making, helping, and nurturing these special individuals to grow.

Life is most fulfilling in the moments you know that you're in the right place, at the right time, doing the right things. We all want the freedom to do *what we want, when we want, how we want, with whomever we want* while *improving the lives of others*.

In this sacred space, it feels like you can achieve anything. Once you experience this kind of flow, you won't forget it! You may spend *years* striving to get back to that sweet spot.

The way forward begins with self-awareness, a commitment to doing no harm, and honest answers to what I call "The Big Questions."

Why am I here?

What is my purpose?

The Role of Faith

Our human nature wants us to know "how" to do it *before we even begin*. What are the steps and how can I do it right? My life experience reminds me of the key scene in *Raiders of the Lost Ark* when Indiana Jones, a man of science, must take a step off a ledge and his father, a man of faith, encourages him to take it, trusting that the step will appear. Indy is, of course, facing a jagged cliff with bottomless darkness below. To find the Holy Grail, the ultimate test of faith is before him. He cannot reason his way through. There is no map, no guarantee he will not plunge to his death. Only darkness lies ahead and below.

But, something inside of him swells up.

Our hero takes that first step.

Viola! The path appears.

Although this is a dramatic example, many of you will relate to the leap of faith required to try new things, to pursue excellence, and to make your own unique path through life and ultimately reach your own holy grail.

I'm here to help you navigate.

I'm here to help you light your fire.

Together, let's answer the most important question for you:

What would you do if you knew you could not fail?

What Does Reaching Your Potential Look Like?

Each and every one of us is a work in progress. Part of the human experience is the hope we all hold inside of reaching our full potential. Yet the fact remains that no one, not Warren Buffet, Richard Branson,

Oprah, Maya Angelou, or Anthony Robbins, has ever reached it. No one has fully, finally *"arrived."*

However, these successful people do have something important in common: contribution.

Remarkable people always give more than they receive. And it's a practice they began well before they were billionaires. Every cliché talks about *enjoying the journey*, but I know with my whole heart that it's more important to actively seek opportunities for generosity, contribution, and beauty in every step. As Wayne Dyer says, "When you change the way you look at things, the things you look at change."

The Hand You've Been Dealt

You've probably heard the notion "everything happens for a reason." I personally don't know why certain things happen. Children become sick, some terminally so. People face catastrophic poverty, heartbreaking accidents and misfortunes every single day. Much of the suffering in the world is beyond my comprehension; the invisible hand of wisdom operating behind the scenes is a matter of personal faith. My faith is in God. But, regardless of how you have arrived here, we all must navigate how to handle difficult circumstances.

I do know this: "It's not what happens to you, but how you react to it that matters." Epictetus, a Greek Stoic philosopher who was born a slave, said these words, and they resonate through time because of their profound truth. Further evidence of finding meaning in suffering can be found in the timeless classic *Man's Search for Meaning* by the Holocaust survivor Viktor Frankl.

As we take the journey together of what to do with the hand you have been dealt, please know that I humbly defer to your religious leaders, philosophers, and spiritual gurus for divine guidance on that topic.

Prodro Pro Tip: *Don't fall into the trap of comparisons.* I hope you are blessed with freedom from extraordinary disabilities or illness. If you are reading this book, I know you have the freedom of the mind. Yet even from this relative place of advantage, you must reach down from deep within for resources. You must continuously cast off perceived limitations. We can *all* mount the seemingly-insurmountable, but no one is exempt from struggle in the pursuit of excellence in service of our passions.

We're going to talk throughout these pages about you deliberately harnessing your human potential. It might get uncomfortable. Why? Because I believe that whatever you are doing right now, *you chose it* to some degree. Personal responsibility and active introspection of your role in creation will provide you the power and ignition to grow beyond your wildest dreams.

Yes, there may have been circumstances that have forced you into a certain kind of work or onto your current path. But you always have a choice about how you perform, pursue, and improve.

I've seen ordinary people perform mightily under extraordinary circumstances, countless times. I believe we are all one, ordinary and extraordinary at the same time.

<u>Prodro Pro Tip:</u> Take a deep breath and reflect as objectively as possible on where you are. Create a non-judgmental inventory of the facts.

Case Study: Jerry is 48 years old. His mom is Spanish and his dad is Asian Indian. He has a degree in business from the University of South Dakota. Jerry worked as a project manager for a Fortune 500 company. His wife was Asian and Native American and worked for herself, running a jewelry company. They had two children who attended public school in North Carolina where the family resided. Jerry wanted to leave the rat race of corporate America but had no idea how. He was mortgaged, leveraged, and committed.

Jerry saw no way out. Jerry was wrong.

He created a vision, shared it with his family, and found performance coaches to help him discover the way. Jerry chose a business idea that he would pursue even if he wasn't paid. A history buff who reads non-stop, Jerry decided to curate collections of history books for private client libraries and sell them online. He took his family to book shows, flea markets, and estate sales where they searched for unique editions of history books for his business. Engaging his family helped with the plan and they enjoyed every minute of it.

Jerry followed a proven go-to-market program he researched. His success was determined by the time and energy he invested in executing the plan. After

24 months, Jerry's new business replaced his income and he left the rat race. Jerry got out. He reinvented himself.

Iterative Improvement

The Japanese word "kaizen" can be translated as "good changes" and reflects a philosophy and belief in the power of incremental, never-ending improvement. Failures and setbacks are to be expected; they are part of a natural and healthy process of constant development. I know this to be true for me. Adversity has deepened my sense of connection and empathy.

In 2007, my husband left our family. I had three children ages five and under. BOOM. It was like an explosion that left a huge crater in its wake. I never thought it could happen to me…and yet, it did. This abandonment was so devastating that the first few years of my life after it happened are now a bit of a blur in my mind.

I was in pure survival mode, even with the support of friends and family. Yet I'm deeply grateful for what happened. I am grateful for the person I have become in the wake of that struggle. My empathy for single parents is profound. My sense of connection with people struggling or rebuilding their lives is off the charts. All that I learned and know today about the balance of hustle and flow was put to the test in a major way. The things I write about in these pages aren't just ideas to me. They are tested, well-worn strategies for thriving when things get tough. Some days were dark; some were full of light and promise. Throughout all of it, I relied on my faith in God to give me the strength to:

- Stand tall to care for my children and myself
- Confront the mountains in front of me
- Hustle to move mountains
- Pray and meditate (flow) to go over, around, or through some mountains
- Ignore some mountains by releasing them, because they were not mine!
- Seek counsel of wise clergy, family, and friends

- Ask for help and stand on the shoulders of strong family, friends, and mentors to leap over a few mountains
- Share my stories to help others… my motivation to write this book

Wherever you stand, whatever your reasons for why you are where you are right now, kaizen and excellence are available to you. This book will give you tips, tools, and real-life stories to help you along your own personal road. I will teach you how to improve incrementally and consistently, and gain resilience to bounce back from setbacks.

The balance between hustle and flow is an unfolding story of navigating through the complex maze of experiences to impact the ultimate outcome of excellence, potential, and enhanced fulfillment in life.

Thank you for the opportunity to share my love and passion for human potential.

Now, let's *light your fire.*

CHAPTER 1 GUIDED JOURNALING EXERCISE

1. How are you spending your precious time, personally and professionally? Is it on something you love and find deeply meaningful?

2. What holds you back?

3. What is your definition of success?

The Big Idea: Lasting motivation comes from within and requires a willingness to be fearlessly authentic. Look within to reveal your own commitment to excellence and never-ending improvement.

CHAPTER 2

WESTERN HUSTLE MEETS EASTERN FLOW: HOW WAYNE DYER CHANGED MY LIFE

> *In order to experience real magic it is necessary to make a dramatic shift from outcome to purpose.* ~Dr. Wayne Dyer

I was a caregiver for my mother as she fought and ultimately passed away from cancer more than 20 years ago. It was the most difficult time of my life.

I loved—and still love—my mother with all of my heart and soul. If there was anything that might have saved her, I tried it. I *hustled* to control everything in my power and many things that weren't. After receiving the opinion (yes, it was only an opinion based on statistics) that she had only a few months to live, we sought a second opinion. A friend referred us to a young oncologist who had saved a friend's life. He looked like the young Dr. Doogie Houser (played by Neil Patrick Harris). We would come to find out that he was wise beyond his years. When we asked him how long she would live, he began acknowledging that he was not God and that answer was between my mom and God. We knew we were in the right place; we were in flow. My mom adored Dr. Cadigan. I drove him crazy faxing over daily lists of questions (yes, that was an actual way of communicating before email, text, and social) about my mother's symptoms, issues, and extensive medications.

I wanted to leave no stone unturned. Was there a supplement, a new shark cartilage treatment, a magical protocol, something overseas that we couldn't access here? I made sure to tell him that no treatment was too expensive. If he found one that could help, we would figure out how to pay for it.

Hustle, hustle, hustle. My brother, sister and I went into overdrive trying to make something happen.

Since I truly believe that miracles happen all the time, I was committed to being in the flow of faith as well, letting a miracle happen to her. So why weren't they happening for my mother? If anyone deserved a miracle cure, it was her. Breathing, meditating, praying, lighting candles, calling on anyone and everyone I could to summon up the power of God and the universe? Yes.

I wanted *more*. I wanted to keep my mom.

Dr. Cadigan was gracious. Every day, he took time to jot down the answers to my questions and dutifully faxed them back. He was trying, in his way, to redirect my energy away from the control and the hustle. I needed, instead, to be with humility in the flow of life, as excruciatingly painful as it was just then.

Meanwhile, Mom and I spent endless hours in the car driving back and forth to chemotherapy and endless doctor's appointments. On these drives, we listened to Wayne Dyer's audio cassette program "Real Magic," in which he speaks about the beauty and serendipity of life. He once said, "Peace is the result of retraining your mind to process life as it is, rather than as you think it should be."

My mother and I loved listening to those tapes together. Instead of focusing on her illness, making small talk, or complaining about other people, we were inspired to speak about what really mattered. It was *real magic* in name and effect; we talked about fear, what in the world we're actually doing here, how energy transitions from one state to another.

Together, we heard and understood that real magic is born of the ways we handle our lives. My mother was not afraid, but I was. She had an unfathomable peace originating in her soul's trust in the never-ending, ultimate, limitless connection we have to God and source.

The Power of Flow

I ultimately came to understand that my mother's miracle would come through in a different way than I expected. I could pray all I wanted. My mother's illness and her covenant with God was between her, her soul, and her Creator. Her miracle was going to be surrendering into her peace with God. She had done her work on the earth. Now she would lead by example, leaving us with an indelible memory of handling illness, life, loss, and pain with extraordinary grace.

Through her countless trips to the doctor's office, she never wavered in her kindness, smile and strength. She greeted each nurse with love and gratitude for their help. At her request, we often baked goodies to bring for the staff or products from our beauty products business, always focusing on bringing joy to others. The staff fussed over Mom's every need and she loved them so deeply.

Even though she was extremely nauseous from the chemo, she insisted on going out for a meal after chemo. I am certain that her body must have felt like it was completely on fire from the inside out, yet she cherished the time being out and chatting with her family members. My mom left every person she met better off than before by asking about them, relating to them, or simply smiling. Her superpower was her zest for life and ability to be in the moment. When she spoke with you, it was as if you were the only human on earth.

Between her example and Wayne Dyer's words, I began to appreciate the magical dance and synergy between the hustle and flow.

The Freedom to CREATE

Shortly before my mother left her body, Wayne Dyer happened to come through town for an evening at the local performing arts center. At this point in my mother's deterioration, there was no question about her ability to attend (as much as she would have loved to). Still, I couldn't wait to see him in person and hear what he had to say. I was grateful beyond measure for all that he had unknowingly contributed to me during my mother's final days.

Wayne's onstage presence was grounded, kind, and powerful.

The Balance Between Hustle & Flow

"If you want to experience prosperity at a miraculous level, you must leave behind your old ways of thinking and develop a new way of imagining what is possible for you to experience in your life," he said.

I heard it loud and clear: I was free to create wildly from an entire world of possibilities—not only financially, but in relationships with loved ones, in living a life of purpose, and passion, and excellence. But first, I had to shift my mindset. I had to learn how to surrender to the universe for me, created by God, and trust that I would receive everything I needed. The peace I received that night was palpable.

At the end of the evening, I rose from my seat, feeling grateful but overwhelmed. A profound channel of sadness was always on in my heart, missing my mom. The crowd loudly streamed out the front door to the lobby for the book signing that followed. I wanted to see Wayne. I wanted to thank him for his contributions to the most difficult time in my life. I felt indebted to him. But right then, the crowds were too much. I missed my mother and longed for her presence there. I needed a moment to process all that I was feeling and thinking before I joined the crowds. I went out the back door, alone.

And there he was, standing next to a table with all of the books on it, also alone. I looked in disbelief because he was "supposed" to be in the front lobby, not there. I could feel his presence and peace emanating from him.

The five minutes we spent alone were some of the most powerful moments of my life.

I told him how meaningful his work was and how it had provided us a structure and language to deal with end-of-life issues, and to fully embrace the beginning of the eternal (aka human death). I explained what he had taught my mother and me about healing relationships, identifying what life is really about for ourselves, and accepting life on its terms as a way to finding peace. I spoke, he listened. When people say "hold space" this is what it felt like, literally.

It struck me that he almost had a physical energy around him that glowed with peace. Soft spoken, yet strong...it reminded me of my mother's presence. He asked, "Where is your mom right now?" and I replied that she was at home, about 10 miles from where we stood. He encouraged me to reach out to her right then and connect with her soul, the part of her goodness and spirit that would remain long after her physical body died. I will never forget praying and connecting with her that moment and all the way home.

I lost track of time and looking back, it was as if God let time stand still for those moments so the crowd would not disturb us. Through some magic, I gained strength from his presence and would later share this experience with my mom, who was grateful and fulfilled in her final days.

This gift of time and attention was powerful not only because of our conversation and the way he held space for me, but because I firmly believe grace, serendipity, and God gave me an unbelievable gift that night. Some event organizers set up a book table in "the wrong place." I stumbled upon it in a completely accidental way, and received precisely what I needed: the courage to believe that even though my mom was going to transition and pass on, I was going to be okay.

The universe and God had my back in ways I hadn't dared believe before. To this day, my greatest wish and hope is that my work in the world will impact your life as meaningfully as he did for ours.

I'm sharing this story with you because in your pursuit of passion and excellence, you *absolutely must* trust in serendipity and a *balance* of hustle and flow. There are times to make things happen and times to let them flow. It is a gift to know the difference.

Foreboding Joy

After meeting Dr. Wayne Dyer and feeling such divine peace about my mom's battle with cancer and the perfect harmony of her soul, I battled with "foreboding joy." This is a concept recently introduced to me by University of Houston's shame and vulnerability researcher, Dr. Brené Brown. I didn't have a name for it back then, but there is solace in knowing I am not alone. It is the fear that creeps in when things are going well—fear the other shoe will drop or that the peace will not last.

I wanted to stay in that divinity, light, and wellness, but our ancient brains have a center of fear called the amygdala. It is designed for survival, but if left unchecked can rob you of the happiness in your life. Combine that with past memories of pain, and a state of anxiety can overcome even the best experience.

It was my job, then, to find a way to honor the peace, stay in the flow, and even hustle past the fear!

The feeling of foreboding joy has indeed never completely left; it attempts to creep into my most precious times even now. It is mastering the balance between hustle and flow that helps me identify, acknowledge and release it.

In the digital age, it is easy to fall into the trap of thinking you must push, push, push all the time to get where you're going. It's rewarded. In some work environments, people who aren't running threadbare are considered somehow less committed or serious. Many believe failure and doom are assured if you don't have proper direction and momentum.

I get it. High energy is my natural state! I was born in New York, raised in Florida, and have a spirited personality type that thrives amid the hustle. It feels like an energetic sizzle: getting up and going, working harder than anybody in the room, being rocket-propelled everywhere I go by an intense internal motivation. I move, I create, I take risks, I clearly see potential in people and situations. This innate drive serves me and my life *abundantly* and I am grateful to all who've appreciated and shared my gregarious perspective over the years.

People have asked me whether hustle (that high-energy, high-spirited innate drive that comes across as gregariousness, spunk, and an outward action-orientation) is the opposite of kindness. Absolutely not. On the contrary, hustle is a form of energy best used in service of kindness, contribution, and service.

An Inspirational Hustler

I recently served as an Executive Producer on a documentary called "Dreamer." During the course of its production, our team headed to New Hampshire to interview one of the main Dreamers. His name is Dean Kamen, and if you have not heard of him (before this film, I had not), he is known as the modern-day Edison for his 400+ patents.

With a great deal of excitement, I prepared and researched Dean's story, life, and accomplishments. It is such a rare gift to be able to have mega-success in commercializing inventions. Dean is that person. He invented the first portable infusion pump in order to help his brother (a physician), then founded AutoSyringe, Inc., to manufacture and market the pump. He sold that company and then founded DEKA Research & Development Corp., where he built a team that created a portable kidney dialysis machine. Today, Dean is best known for inventing the Segway scooter.

For the interview portion of the Dreamer documentary, Dean invited our team into his home. To paint a little picture of how extraordinary he is as a human, you should know there is a steam engine in his foyer and a helipad on his property. The multiple levels of his home are filled with inventions, awards, and insights into true human potential.

The day left me speechless. Anyone that knows me will confirm that this is unbelievable. Dean's sincere desire to help humanity and solve real problems changed the fundamental way I think. Contribution. It's a theme that comes up over and over when you take a closer look at hustle and flow.

Dean Kamen sees a problem and approaches it from different angles. He told the story of inventing the iBot, a wheelchair that can climb stairs and raise you up to a standing position. It all began when he went to the mall and saw a man in a wheelchair attempting to get up a curb without assistance. Next, he saw the same man in the store attempting to pay but he could not reach the counter. "I realized at that moment that people in wheelchairs do not have a mobility problem, they have a dignity problem," Dean said.

The rest is history. Dean Kamen invented the iBot wheelchair that created independence and the ability for its users to raise up to a standing position for the National Anthem, to shake hands, to pay a cashier, or simply to climb a curb or stair.

In the course of this life-changing day, my mind and my mouth were in a constant race. Hustle, ask questions, contemplate and listen, flow. If you had my brain wired up and could peek at its activity, I am certain you would have seen that new neural pathways being formed. My excitement and engagement were off the charts, even for me. Dean was so calm and natural in telling his stories of innovation, motivation, overcoming challenges and unparalleled success. He wore jeans and a jean shirt and had salt and pepper hair and was late to our interview because he had come from a meeting with the Department of Defense and Bill Gates.

There was a moment in our one-on-one conversation when I asked what was next or what his dream project would be. He responded that time travel is the only way he could accomplish solving all the big problems he was working on. *Time.* That is his weakness and from what I experienced it is really his only one.

At that moment, I felt a certain compassion and connection to Dean, knowing that we had something profoundly important in common.

We both had to decide how to spend our precious time on Earth.

Dean founded a non-profit called FIRST: For the Recognition of Science and Technology. His legacy of treating science and technology champions like rock stars and world-class athletes has forever changed the world. Be sure to check out our documentary by the Emmy Award-Winning Producer Nick Nanton for the rest of Dean Kamen's story!

Balance

There is certainly a cost if your hustle is unbalanced. Push your way through life relentlessly and blindly, and eventually you're going to miss the signs. You're going to blow right through your exit, and if you're not careful, cause real harm to yourself or others.

At one of the pivot points of my life, I was feeling overworked, overstressed and like I was in complete hustle mode. Working with a tech startup was intense and invigorating but it was as if the energy was starting to become friction. Can you relate? What was once a driving, thriving passion started to become a duty and paycheck. I wasn't on the same wavelength with the CEO. Yet I was full-throttle…without much of an exit plan.

One Friday evening, I stopped in the local liquor store to buy a nice bottle of wine. I had planned to do some soul searching at home by myself that night. It was a small, locally-owned store that I frequented weekly for wine for family parties and visiting friends. The man who worked there knew my preference for California chardonnay, J. Lohr or Cakebread. He was always there and always helpful. That particular evening, I was preoccupied but remember saying "Hi!" as I walked in. I headed to the familiar chardonnay shelves; I didn't need help and someone else was checking out at the time.

On the white wine shelf, right at my eye level, sat a bottle of red wine. Yes, red wine out of place on the white wine shelf.

I instinctively picked it up and looked at the label: "Prospero" was the name of the vineyard; the label was adorned with an image of Greek columns. $27.99. At just that moment, another man came around the corner. It was just the two of us there and he said, "Hello, what is that red wine doing over here?"

"I don't know," I replied, "but the strange thing is Prospero is the name of my dad's business."

I was a bit in awe and disbelief. I had never seen this winery before; certainly, I would have noticed it. My father's name was Spero Prodromitis and the company was a form of his name ProSpero. Add the uncanny fact that the bottle had Greek columns on it (we are, of course, Greek). I'm not sure how long our conversation went on, but the man said, "I want you to have it."

I nodded, said "thank you," and grabbed a bottle of chardonnay as well and headed to check out. The man I knew rang me up for the chardonnay and bagged both bottles. Looking at the receipt later, I realized I wasn't charged for the Prospero wine. The remarkable thing is I never saw the second man tell the cashier he gifted it to me. I was emotional about this turn of events, as you can imagine. It was a difficult time in my life and my father had died when I was eight. I could have used his sage advice about what to do next.

I went home and stared at the bottle of Prospero red wine while sipping a nice glass. I looked up the winery, half expecting to see that my dad was a part owner or some other obvious sign. I found nothing more than the name and Greek columns (as if that wasn't enough). But I couldn't let it go. My curiosity led me to return to the store in the next few days and talk to the gentleman I knew there. He said they didn't carry that winery, Prospero.

When I asked about the man who gave me the $27.99 bottle of red wine for free, he looked puzzled.

"No one else worked here that night. No one fitting that description is even affiliated with our store. Are you sure it was here and not another store? I worked alone on Friday night."

I was silent and politely said, "Thank you."

I barely made it to the car before tears started rolling down my face. It was an angel; it could have even been my father. I was so caught up in hustle that I almost missed the most important sign of my life.

A few months later, I left that job and went into business with my brother. He told me he had registered a business name for us earlier that year.

Yes, the name was Prospero.

We have been extremely blessed and successful.

Photo caption: Mary and Spero Prodromitis, Mommy and Daddy

The Art of Receiving

The flow is taking a step back and becoming aware. It is a practice of taking a breath, opening, actually listening, receiving, trusting, surrendering. Flow is quiet. Flow *allows* life to happen without needing to control it. The fabric of time is suspended here.

Flow is the willingness to be led by the current of something larger than you, which will ultimately take you in *its* chosen direction. It is a divinely designed balance that acknowledges the limits of one's human power and capacity. In this space, we find wisdom through paying attention to the signs. We know intuitively we are on the right path.

In the space of flow, synchronicity is available to enact miracles and move you forward in unexpected ways. Previously unknown and unthinkable opportunities come to you there, in the flow, as if they were divinely directed. We find ourselves supported in ways we never could have orchestrated for ourselves.

I was lucky enough to inherit my parents' Zen-like strength, and have learned to harness and work with it over time. You can do this, too.

What a beautiful art, the ability to skillfully wield transformative energy to *make* things happen with excitement, enthusiasm, passion, and drive—and then pivot into silence, into mindful, caring attention that allows life to move through you.

This is the way of mastery and excellence.

The space between hustle and flow is where real magic happens in my life. Their balance is my source of tremendous success, fulfillment, happiness, and peace during difficult times.

Everything Is Energy

Energy is the fabric that holds every molecule in the universe together. Energy gets you up in the morning and keeps you down when you don't feel well. You eat lunch and the miracle of your human body converts that salad, burger, or banana into energy. Energy is what people exchange in positive and negative ways. You feel it, even if you can't always express it satisfactorily. Energy is the physical strength and force of life.

Scientists in France working on alternative continuous energy sources led us to an understanding of molecular fusion, a process that separates two molecules and then drives them back together with great force. It requires so much energy that they had to take out all carbon-based walls and replace them with beryllium and tungsten. Scientists are optimistic, but they are just beginning, and for now the process takes in more energy than is available at output. In other words, it costs more than it creates.

This is a perfect analogy for the early stages of any new development, particularly business ventures. To thrive in your life with passion and excellence, you need energy, a *lot* of it. But you must learn discernment about when to go full throttle and when to ease back and balance out your horizon. Passion will help you light your fire, but if you want to build something that lasts, you will need a source of fuel that continues a slow burn without depleting your energy over time.

I have never known anyone in my life who has more purpose driven energy than my brother Dean. He went to work as a young teen when our father died and learned to balance school, sports and work. He never complained and he defined hustle early in his life.

Dean is one of those charismatic people everyone wants to be around. In high school, he was voted "most humorous" and was a star football player. He turned down a college football scholarship to stay local and help support our family. Balanced with his hustle is his profound sense of purpose and duty. They are so seamless that Dean also epitomizes the flow we are discussing. Our relationship has led us to own multiple businesses together and support each other in balancing the hustle and flow. It is such a great lesson for me to be reminded that I did not get here on my own. Surround yourself with like-minded, amazing humans and you will improve your life exponentially!

Prodro Pro Tip: Make a list of ten activities, thoughts, people, or things that give you energy. Keep the list where you can see it (perhaps on your phone or on your bathroom mirror). Then, if you need a lift, look at the list and pick one of the things on it. My list includes:

- 10-minute centering meditation
- Brisk walk on the treadmill
- Calling my best friend on the phone
- Watching a Les Brown or Tony Robbins YouTube Video on Motivation
- Enjoying a cup of coffee, out on my patio in nature
- Writing in a gratitude journal
- Looking through the smile box gift from my children (full of all the things they love about me)
- Standing up from my desk and imagining how it feels to win the Lotto! (true story, you can ask my kids, lol)

CHAPTER 2 GUIDED JOURNALING EXERCISE

1. **My narrative of how my life "should be" is:**

2. **I know it is time to push (hustle) when I feel:**

3. **I know it is time to let things happen (flow) when I feel:**

The Big Idea: The first step to creating more meaning and fulfillment in your life is to honor your relationship with hustle and flow. No matter where you are in life, there is a balance between making things happen and letting them flow. Practice, notice, and refine your skills.

PART II

A LOOK WITHIN

CHAPTER 3

THE FIRST INFLUENCE: FAMILY & EARLY BEGINNINGS

The quest for balance is universal but the perfect balance is a myth. -Randi Zuckerberg

There is a scene in the movie *My Big Fat Greek Wedding* that I think about often. The main character Toula is talking to her mother. Toula is extremely distraught because her father will not allow her to take computer classes. In a heavy Greek accent, her mother responds with words both memorable and wise: "The man might be the head of the household, but the woman is the neck."

The neck can turn the head any way she wants. With her mother's crafty intervention, Toula is soon off to school, changing her life for good.

How has an early experience or set of beliefs influenced your life?

I learned early in life to never underestimate where I was, or the power I had to change the minds of people around me.

At a young age, I read the book *Psycho-Cybernetics* by Maxwell Maltz. In the book, a cosmetic surgeon learns the physical beauty he can create with surgery does not heal the internal negative self-image of his patients. Wow. What a powerful insight! My early exposure to success literature and personal development books had a huge impact on me. Learning about the power of the subconscious mind and the importance of putting positive intentions forward shaped me in profound ways.

Photo caption: Themie Prodromitis (sister), Mary Prodromitis (mom), Spero Prodromitis (dad), Theo Prodromitis (me in front, the baby), and Dean Prodromitis (brother).

One of the greatest gifts I have ever received was being raised in a family that holds ideas, concepts, and conversation as sacred. My family and early upbringing taught me the following concept.

Leap Before You're Ready

On some average day early in the third grade, a fateful announcement came over the intercom. School administrators needed someone to run the school store. Were there any takers? I nearly leapt out of my chair, one arm in the air and the other pushing its elbow to maximum reach.

It could have been all my volunteer time after school banging out Mrs. Clark's erasers, or the fact that it was only my hand reaching up with such enthusiasm, but my name was called. I grabbed the hall pass and speed-walked directly to the front office, mentally preparing to elbow my way in line to apply for the job of school store manager.

When I arrived in the front office, I looked to the left and I looked to the right. There was no one else in line. This couldn't be right; no one else was seizing this prized opportunity? But the front office secretary looked down and said, "Oh hello, Theo. I'd love to show you the school store."

All through the previous year I had arrived at school early to stand in a long line that wrapped around the cafeteria. I was a diehard devotee of the Sunset Hills supply store. In the days before Staples or Office Depot, students had fewer options and rarely missed a chance to purchase special paper, pencil, or erasers. The school store had an air of magic and possibility.

The "store" structure was simple and wonderful: just a metal rack on wheels with several shelves and a locking door on the front to protect its coveted treasures. There was a real metal cash box that I would command. I was elated to be entrusted with so much. Even more than that, I was highly motivated by the prospect of being the center of attention. In front of the whole school, I got to see and greet everyone first thing in the morning. I vowed to be there bright and early, and to make magic happen.

The most important part was that my parents were proud of me. A family of seasoned business people, we sat at the dinner table and discussed my commitment to getting to school early and collaborated on invaluable sales strategies that still serve me today:

1) Focus on the customer. Sales is *not* just trying to tell customers everything you know.
2) A sincere compliment can break the ice much better than "Can I help you?" or, "Are you looking for something?"
3) Ask genuine questions: A great question about someone's needs will match the right product and customer.
4) Relax: It is okay not to sell to every single person.
5) Upselling is great, and it won't feel pushy if the product is right for the customer.

I was wildly successful, breaking all kinds of sales records of pencils, erasers, and protractors. Children lined up to see the store's wares, and many left with far more than they intended, just because we had fun. I was inspired and on fire. I discovered what it felt like to be completely in my element.

Both my mom and dad were happy to take me to school early and lauded my successes. I had no way of knowing it was an important time to leap before I was ready. Later that year, my father died. I have always cherished the knowledge that when he died, he was proud of me and I had lessons to take with me for a lifetime.

Manifestation

By 1990, all of my family's early influence came to beautiful fruition in my career. At that time, I was working in our family's business. My amazing cousin George had opened (and my brother Dean later took over) a wholesale beauty supply company called Total Image, serving salons in Florida. It involved big fashion and hair shows, beauty trends, sales, accounting and grit. My marketing, oversight, operational and product expertise was growing. My role evolved and since I was family, I performed any job needed from receptionist, to show model to researcher to order packing. What I still credit George with decades later is his commitment to excellence in every detail. He set an example and inspired me to great heights. I am forever grateful for his tenacity and contribution to my professional development.

By that time, I had already invested in personal development and knew that I could actively create the life I wanted. Even though it was well before the heyday of psycho-spiritual Law of Attraction manifestation techniques, I understood implicitly that I had to ask for what I wanted, trust God and the universe, and then let it go. I had the Greek hustle down and was fine tuning the flow.

Here is my highly recommended, proven strategy for getting what you want:

I took out a piece of paper and wrote down my intention: to work in a positive environment with freedom to travel while making a certain amount each year. I dreamed up what my life would look like in that scenario. I wrote these intentions, then I spoke them out loud with gratitude. I sealed them in an envelope and let it go. I decided to follow the flow, to let the universe bring it to fruition. I asserted that I would be guided to the right opportunities and next steps, and then released it.

Soon after, I got a call from a manufacturer's rep affiliated with our family business. He said that he was leaving his job. I would be a perfect replacement, if I would just interview for it, he said. How flattering! But I had never been to a professional interview before. What was I going to wear? How was this going to happen? I didn't have a resume. I didn't know where to begin. It was daunting and sudden and I was tempted to jump back into the self-doubt, fear of the unknown, and chaos.

Yet, I had asked for it. I set an intention without attachment, and it was now up to me to harness my hustle and turn an opportunity into gold. I wasn't ready, but it was time to leap. Looking back, I'd never have come so far without that first initial act of faith.

Many years later, when my mother died. I found the original, unopened letter. The details had all manifested down to the most specific detail.

Do you have a story of hustle and flow that reminds you of your role in creating your life?

Prodro Pro Tip: Write down your goals and intentions for the year ahead. State them in the positive, "I am so happy and grateful now that…." and list every detail. Feel the deepest sense of happiness and emotion as if it was already manifest. This practice can take time but your mind does not know the difference between real and imagined events if the emotion is strong enough. God and the universe will conspire to figure out the details to make it happen. Hustle to write & feel it. Then, flow and let it go.

It All Falls Apart: Embracing the Rhythm of Life

There are inevitably times when you will feel like you are in an alternate universe. Like you are on a different plane of reality than nearly everyone else in your life. This is the most ignored part of the journey in most success stories. I have often marveled at the crisis-to-success leap. What happened in the middle of the story?

When I have been "stuck," I resort to doing 10 things in the hustle to make things happen and meditating or sitting quietly for 10 days in a row afterward to give flow a chance to kick in. This is the absolute essence of the balance I teach others.

Anthony Robbins asks, "What is one step you could take for massive action?"

Me: "I don't know"

AR: "But, if you *did* know, what would you do?"

Me: "I would probably call an expert or ask a friend, or research on the internet."

The point is that we don't have to have all the answers, we just have to work through it, and take action. Do *something*.

Some people cannot calm the chatter in the mind or meditate. But all that is required is to sit quietly for 10 minutes a day for 10 days in a row. I recommend doing so first thing in the morning. When you first wake up, your brain operates at around 10.5 waves per second. The range from eight to 13 Hz, or cycles per second, is the alpha stage. It's been called the gateway to the subconscious mind. You don't have to "do" anything. Just notice the thoughts popping up and release them. If you are able to say a mantra or just sit in gratitude, that's perfect. YouTube has a ton of content from Dr. Wayne Dyer, Bob Proctor, Louise Hay, Dr. Deepak Chopra and more free resources if you want music or a guide to your quiet time.

During periods of life when you are rebuilding, breaking old patterns, or forging new territory, the need for hustle and flow are more acute. When it comes down to survival (as it will eventually for all of us), you'll need them both more than ever.

CHAPTER 3 GUIDED JOURNALING EXERCISE

1. The best things and the most challenging things about my family are:

2. My family would describe me as:

3. **Who is the first person you tell when something great happens? Who do you go to for support when you face a big hurdle? Why?**

The Big Idea: We constantly repeat unconscious patterns that were greatly influenced by our families. Set yourself free with an honest assessment of how this aspect of your experience influences your self-concept, goals, and life balance.

CHAPTER 4

THE SECOND INFLUENCE: YOUR INTERPERSONAL ENVIRONMENT: RELATIONSHIPS

We are the average of the five people we spend the most time with. ~Jim Rohn

We are social mammals who live our lives in concentric circles. The company you keep *absolutely* shapes your belief in your potential, your goals, and ultimately what you are able to achieve in life. Taking an objective look at how your circles influence your life and goals may surprise you.

It definitely surprised me.

I started reading articles, blogs and posts from Randi Zuckerberg a few years ago. I loved her perspective, spirit and bold tenacity. She was one of the first employees at her brother's company Facebook; she was in Marketing and created Facebook Live. She was also the sibling that *graduated* from Harvard. (insert smiley face). She conquered the West coast hustle in Silicon Valley and was often the only woman in the room.

She chose flow when she departed Facebook to accept a starring role in a Broadway show called *Rock of Ages*. Are you feeling the total leap of faith it must've taken to follow her lifelong passion for the arts? Risk-taker extraordinaire. The press was less than kind to her, only to eat their words as she gracefully accepted two Tony Awards in 2019.

Randi's company, Zuckerberg Media, promotes women in tech and opportunities for females to be included in decision-making. Her accomplishments are too numerous to list, but a children's book *Dot Complicated*, and my favorite book called *Pick Three* are a few that I must mention.

Randi, to put it mildly, is my kind of woman!

I earned the opportunity to join Zuckerberg Institute, which mentors entrepreneurs and ultimately met Randi in person. It was life changing. As an entrepreneur, artist and innovator, being around this woman, who is also a dedicated wife and mother of three, influenced me to eliminate any lingering limits to my goals and dreams. In other words, being around Randi gave me permission to soar. She showed me a strength and grace that I can only attempt to describe. She is authentic, tenacious, and loving all at once.

I write about Randi here because simply being in her presence *changed* me. Read that sentence again. In this chapter we are going to think about whose presence you are in most often and how it influences you.

Let's take a step back, here, and consider your big goals. It's fashionable to say that 95 percent of people don't set goals and therefore don't achieve them; that goal setting is a habit unique to the highest-performing people. But goals can mean different things to different people. What are they for you? Write them down. Then, get ready to see how these goals are affected by your people.

Bring to mind the five most influential people in your life—in this case, defined as *those with whom you spend the most time, excluding your children*. Yes, there may be other very influential people in your life you see less regularly. But for now, focus on the *daily* conversations, interactions, relationships you surround yourself with, whether by choice or default.

First: Take an inventory of who inhabits your closest circles for the most amount of time. For one week, observe and log who you're spending most of your time with, whether in person, by phone, or through text/email—just to get a sample. If you spend less than 20 minutes per day with a person, they may not qualify.

Second: Notice what you're talking about or what you're doing when you're spending time with each person. Work associates count even if they are not with you all the time. When you start to see negative patterns of interaction, it may be tempting to write them off, believing that you aren't overly affected. Most of us think, "Oh, I can handle it." We are certain we are stronger than whatever energy or intention is being put on us.

"It's just who they are, and it's not hurting me," we think, when we consider that family member, the neighbor, or colleague. Well, maybe. And it may also be true that the energy you are soaking up, like photosynthesis, isn't in line with your personal goals and hopes. The company you keep may be contributing to a *one step forward, two steps back* phenomenon many of us experience at some point.

For example, if you work in a cubicle and are seated next to somebody who is inherently negative or doesn't believe in your potential (or the possibility of happiness or advancement for anyone), they could be rubbing off on you in ways you don't immediately notice.

Third: Honestly assess the alignment between the amount and quality of time you spend with others and how that time contributes to where *you* want to go. How much nourishment are you routinely experiencing when it comes to moving toward your goals? Are you free to begin creating the version of yourself you'll need to become to get to the next level? How do the people around you react when you share a new idea, goal, or pursuit? When you say, "I need to carve out some serious time this week to work on my goals," or "I'm going to the gym," or "I signed up to attend a workshop. You'll have to go to lunch without me this week," do you enjoy support? Or do you experience attempts to "protect you" from failure or shove you back into the box they are comfortable with you being in?

Expect some resistance to the status quo. It is worth it to curate your own life and time.

By no means am I suggesting you cut people out of your life. But remember that your time and energy are limited. You are the only one who directs your life force. Perhaps you need to limit your time in some areas and redirect it appropriately.

I found an honest review of the five people I spend the most time with to be wonderful and very telling at the same time. It gave me a chance to see how my goals, achievements, and potential were developing.

It's not easy, but I continue to make choices that support my passion and commitment to serving with excellence.

What can *you* do?

Prodro Pro Tip: Practice shutting down or redirecting toxic or negative conversations.

Family can be difficult here. It is a hard truth that our closest family members may not be overly supportive of our goals, either because they want to protect us from failure or have some other ulterior motive. Even when the impulse behind an interaction is loving and compassionate, the end result can still be limiting and potential-stifling. So yes, let's acknowledge that daring to dream big with your immediate family can sometimes feel even more like a risk of getting laughed at or rejected by strangers. Be ready.

Rejection

No matter who you are or how you are working to reach your potential, you are going to experience rejection. Whether it's by one of the five people closest to you, a family member, a colleague, or a prospective client. We all experience this, and no one likes it. But to pursue excellence while managing the balance between hustle and flow in your life, you'll need to develop some mastery here. It is a critical point.

The difficult truth is that the closer you get to your peak performance, the more opportunities for rejection will emerge, both personally and professionally. If you are pushing your limits, there *will* come a time when you feel rejected. It could happen first thing in the morning with your family. You're hustling to get the day started, and boom, a sideways comment about your work schedule lands like a punch. Rejection from those closest to you often feels the most hurtful.

On to work, where the vulnerability of all of the business relationships, friendships, and connections is a ripe environment for rejection. Eight to 10 hours a day is a lot of time to spend with anyone; there are endless opportunities here for someone to throw shade on your ideas, your hopes, or the contribution you are trying to make. Sometimes it is hard to separate out what's actually being rejected: is it *you*? Is it your ideas? Your approach to the work?

The question for us now is what to do in the face of rejection so you continue to grow along your path of passion and excellence. You're going to embody your fully-realized potential.

So, let's take inventory of your personal toolkit for handling rejection.

First, get clear about ways you can handle rejection on the personal level (from friends, family, intimate colleagues) differently from rejection you may experience professionally. Your responses to each situation may share a common thread, but an emotional, personal rejection *is not the same* as someone who isn't on board with a business idea. Because you are a human mammal, they may *feel* the same - but your toolbox needs different tools to cope with these objectively different experiences.

So, what is your default response to a perceived rejection?

When someone has offended you with their words, actions, or the way they look at you, do you snark at them? Do you retreat inward, pushing the hurt down and internalizing it? Do you have a habit of believing critical things people say about you because they are easier to accept than compliments?

How does your default response to rejection or criticism support or detract from your ability to be powerful and in the balance of hustle and flow?

- Does it support your goals?
- Does it veer you way off track?
- Do you reflexively cut ties?
- Or have you cultivated the skillset to turn difficult situations into learning experiences?
- What are you *choosing* to do, say, or create during moments of rejection?

Prodro Pro Tip: You always have a choice. You can turn *any* situation into a growth opportunity. Practice responding in a neutral manner to unpleasant personal and professional statements or actions. My best advice is to respond with, "That's interesting" when you are surprised or at a loss for words. You can even follow up with "I'm curious; tell me more about why you said that." Information is power, and the ability to gather data with an open mind is powerful.

Cultivating Resilience

Studies show that we have one set of responses at the ready for personal rejection, and one set for the workplace. We tend to stick with whatever we have defaulted to for many, many years. In Brené Brown's book *Rising Strong*, she says that resilience is built on our willingness to experience discomfort and get familiar with all of our feelings, even the negative ones.

The best way to handle rejection is to create resilience, to preserve your ability to function so it won't eat up your creativity bandwidth or veer you off track. Here are some strategies:

- Reach out to someone you trust who can hold space for your feelings of rejection. Complaining to your friends or your mother may feel like a release, and sometimes venting is helpfully cathartic. But don't stop here. The most powerful companions in this arena will empathize and normalize your painful feelings of rejection, rather than your victimization.
- If you are likely to internalize rejection, try something that's grounding and comforting to you. Sit with a cup of hot tea at the beach. Take a breath and a bath. Ask someone to rub your shoulders or feet. Note that your actions may be rejected, not you.
- If you are likely to lash out and respond with anger, go for a run. Go to the gym and hit a punching bag, use your body to physically channel all of the reactivity into healthy action. Tony Robbins advocates changing your emotional state quickly through movement.

Above all, remember that *any* rejection, no matter how personal it feels, is more telling about the other person, what's happening within them and what they're putting out. It is never truly about you, no matter how it feels.

In his classic book *The Four Agreements*, Don Miguel Ruiz teaches: "As you make a habit of not taking anything personally, you won't need to place your trust in what others do or say. You will only need to trust yourself to make responsible choices. You are never responsible for the actions of others; you are only responsible for you. When you truly understand this, and refuse to take things personally, you can hardly be hurt by the careless comments or actions of others."

What I'd like you to create is your own personal resilience plan. Your plan is made up of many different micro and macro strategies, all with the aim of clearing out distractions and maintaining your bandwidth, to open channels for abundance and goodness. For our purposes, bandwidth is defined as the mental and emotional capacity required to hustle when you want to and flow when you need to.

A standard rejection response is one of the most important tools in your resilience plan, helping you build the rejection-tolerance muscle and effectiveness in reaching your goals.

And what *one magical ingredient* makes all of this unfold with ease and grace?

Forgiveness.

Prodro Pro Tip: Practice shutting down or redirecting toxic or negative conversations. How will I do that?

Prodro Pro Tip: You always have a choice. You can turn *any* situation into a growth opportunity. Practice responding in a neutral manner to unpleasant personal and professional statements or actions.

CHAPTER 4 GUIDED JOURNALING EXERCISE

1. **The 5 people that I spend the most time with are:**

   -
   -
   -
   -
   -

2. **Their beliefs about me include:**

3. **This influences me by:**

The Big Idea: Achieving a life of freedom to pursue one's own vision and goals requires a tough look at our circle of influence. It is not always easy to release our inner circle from inadvertently directing our course. But it is a worthwhile endeavor to hustle without needing permission and to flow when you know it is right.

CHAPTER 5

THE THIRD INFLUENCE: MINDSET

Once your mindset changes, everything on the outside will change along with it. ~Steve Maraboli, Life, Truth and Being Free

To achieve anything close to your full potential, you must harness the gift of *presence*. It's simple, but it's not easy...and it's not negotiable: you must cultivate the ability to focus on what is right in front of you. Begin by moving your baggage out of the way. Develop habits that release old, unresolved stories and find access to new energy, clarity, and capacity.

Forgiveness

Every single human on earth benefits from the lessons we learn from forgiveness. What does forgiveness have to do with achieving your goals? A lot. Just as rejection clogs up your bandwidth, a mind and heart consumed with anger and resentment have *zero* growth potential. There's no space. You're maxed out. All of your hustle is going to be directed (whether in obvious or subtle ways) to finding a way to get back at your persecutor. To make them pay.

As we journey into this crucial topic, however, please don't mistake forgiveness with permission. Whether you've got someone on the chopping block for a microlevel rejection/infraction or a truly deep hurt, your achieving forgiveness *does not condone* what happened. It doesn't lessen the pain of the injury. It doesn't give them a pass to continue harmful behavior.

> *"Forgiveness is the fragrance that the violet sheds*
> *on the heel that has crushed it."*
> ~Mark Twain (attributed)

But if your precious life energy is spent hustling to prove them wrong, to make others see their flaws, or get back at them, *you will never find the flow that you need to grow.* Serendipity won't show up for you in miraculous and helpful ways.

Yes, reaching a state of forgiveness is easier said than done. The first step is deciding that whatever hurt you is no longer permitted to take up so much space in your life. It may no longer dictate what your mind and heart focus on. Your future and endeavors are more important than your grudges.

Good.

Next, develop a micro-strategy for forgiving small infractions that happen on a daily basis. Micro-rejections. Rudeness. Thoughtless comments. Bad drivers. It takes some time to develop a habit, but once you do, you are widening your own potential in this arena. This is not to say that small hurts don't sting. Of course they do! Allow that to hurt for a few minutes, breathe, and then do your best to visualize letting go of whatever resentment came up with the pain.

You will find plenty of opportunities to practice the skill of forgiveness. You may be surprised by how many times forgiveness comes up in a day: ten, a hundred times, every thirty seconds? You'll first notice the constant need to autocorrect. Start to notice how you tell yourself a story of what happened, where you put it in your mental files, and how much time and energy you give it.

Forgiving Yourself

Next, I want to challenge you to develop an even tougher habit: routinely forgiving yourself. Developing an active strategy for forgiving yourself is absolutely critical.

No matter how noble and well intentioned, I am human. The struggle is real to forgive myself daily for either not eating healthy or wasting time (yes, wasting it scrolling on social media).

"It wasn't personal. Things happen. I did the best I could with what I had, and that's life. I can do better next time. I'm deserving and worthy of this."

That is an example of a helpful inner dialogue in the wake of a mistake. Does it sound like your own inner voice, or does it sound like a foreign language? Think about it.

I have a quick wit and sometimes speak before thinking. Then, I feel horrible about it. One of my close friends was going through a grueling divorce. She and I saw a movie together and she had a visceral reaction to the main character (a bad guy). In one of my dumbest moments, I told her that she thought all men were bad because of her ex-husband. Oof. Who says that? I felt awful for saying it. It was unnecessary, unkind, and probably untrue. It took me some time to really forgive myself (even after calling her to apologize profusely). The sting was hard to shake that I had hurt someone I love.

What's your daily micro-strategy for being kind to yourself? You will find that a stronger self-forgiveness muscle makes it easier to forgive those around you, a nice side effect. Once you've developed the habit, forgiveness of both self and others comes so much easier. Just this one habit can actually generate more of the positive energy you need to hustle, flow, and thrive.

A word about the hard things: loss of loved ones, relationships, getting passed over for a promotion, or personal harm. Sometimes we can integrate these life experiences by turning our attention to them and recognizing there's a bigger picture. However, often we just get *stuck*. We play a record of something painful over and over again, and reach the point of being unable to handle it on our own. Trauma creates physiological patterns that keep us in a vicious loop. During these times, there is absolutely no shame in reaching out for the support of mental and emotional health professionals. Move the experience into an adaptive center of the brain with help from those who know how.

Explore Alternative Therapies

Consider seeking professional help with non-invasive therapies like EMDR and Baud Sound that move your thoughts themselves to an adaptive part of your brain. EMDR (Eye Movement Desensitization and Reprocessing) is a psychotherapy that can help people to heal from the symptoms and emotional distress that are the result of trauma. Scientific studies show that by using EMDR therapy, people can experience the benefits of psychotherapy in just a few sessions that once took years to make a difference.[2]

The beauty of EMDR lies in the non-intrusive use of eye movement to mobilize emotional memories and move them from a non-adaptive place in the brain to an adaptive center. The results can happen faster than the traditional multi-year therapy required for all kinds of issues. EMDR was developed for Post Traumatic Stress Disorder (PTSD) and expanded for clinical use to treat everyday depression, emotional trauma, and bullying. Trigger events are desensitized by a methodology of accessing and moving memories. There are numerous studies and a 25-year history of success. In many cases, after the EMDR therapeutic process, people's thoughts, feelings and behavior indicate improved emotional health.

BioAcoustical Utilization Device (BAUD Therapy) is somewhat similar. It uses earphones and frequencies to activate neural pathways and disrupt patterns. Like a groove in a record, these pathways to emotional pain can be modulated with sound. It is amazing to see the results of working within the brain without medication to effect long term relief.

I have had both EMDR and BAUD, and they are significant. I love the non-invasive nature and efficacy of these methods, which can take as few as 10-15 sessions for lasting change.

Self-Talk and the Judgment Train to Nowhere

Theodore Roosevelt wrote these words to his friend William Sturgis Bigelow on March 29, 1898: *Comparison is the thief of joy.* I couldn't agree more. Self-awareness is a gift that comes with tremendous responsibility

---

[2] https://www.emdr.com/what-is-emdr/ Accessed April, 2020.

to be kind to ourselves. The reality is that your beliefs and the way you manage inner dialogue run the show, 24/7. And depending on how your mind and heart have been trained, some of the most damaging, relentless, hurtful comments come from inside.

This constant inner chatter affects our lives in countless drastic ways. It determines what we take action on—and how. The inner narrative also determines our potential: what we believe ourselves to be capable of and what may be possible for our lives. While positive self-talk and affirmations also work with subconscious programming, for the sake of our work let's stay at the level of the self-talk that you can control. This includes what you say and what you hear when you get up in the morning and walk past the mirror.

A majority of people wake up to judgment and critical thoughts about themselves and those around them: "The kids are making me late *again*? My boss is going to kill me. I'm not cut out for this. When will people realize that I don't actually deserve it? I'm such a mess."

Yikes.

What you say to yourself about yourself is everything. Is the conversation self-deprecating from the first moment of the day onward? Is it largely a critical voice? Can you hear a voice of kindness and generosity too? Do you hear quiet at some points more than others?

Your inner dialogue goes with you everywhere you go, including to work and to business situations. When you're in a meeting, how often are you fully there? Are you hearing what others say, in their words, body language, and actions? If you're too focused on yourself, you're missing important things.

The most peaceful space is when you're in flow and the inner voice is not talking about yourself or another person. Clarity arrives when you're actually just *present*. Meditation and other mindfulness techniques may help you develop the self-talk control muscle.

You have your own angel and little devil on your shoulder, and they're always engaged in a battle for your attention. But no one can force themselves to think a certain way. Even in deep meditation the thoughts return like the tides. Even the most successful people among us have inner chatter. So, what can we do?

Start just as experienced meditators do: simply notice the thoughts.

Be willing to take a hard look at what you actually say about yourself during the course of the day. When you notice negative self-talk, gently interrupt it. Bring to mind an experience and evidence to the contrary of what it's saying. Input enough positive information to stack the deck in your favor. Fill yourself up with enough positive references, memories of meeting many small goals, so that affirming self-talk will be backed up by experience.

> *When you wake up in the morning, give yourself a good leader mirror test. If you look like you're going to be a sulking, pouting bore, slap yourself in the face before you go out to the office.*
> *~tough love from Jack Welch[3]*

What about "Fake it 'till you make it?" While there is a case for putting your best foot forward, denying the truth will never change what's going on. Only self-awareness, kindness toward yourself, and a commitment to align your habits with your goals can do that.

The center of every conversation—even the ones you are constantly having with yourself—is meaning.

As you stop to listen to your self-talk, you will likely notice how much of it concerns comparisons between yourself and others. Social media is your nemesis in this regard, as it gives the illusion that everybody else is doing better than you. Many wellness studies, including those cited by Dr. Laurie Santos at Yale University in her popular course Psychology and the Good Life, demonstrate that as we increase time spent on social media, we feel worse about ourselves.

So, while comparison may be a natural human habit, notice where you go overboard with it. There is uniqueness and beauty in what you have been through in life. No one else has walked the path the way you have, and when you find ways to soften all of the judgment and change your tone toward yourself—even modestly; aim for just a 10% improvement—you will drastically transform your productivity, your happiness, and your balance of energy. With more positive self-talk, you will find the flow easier to access. And when you hustle, it will be with more confidence.

---

[3] https://jackwelch.strayer.edu/winning/mirror-test-leader/ Accessed April, 2020.

Prodro Pro Tip: If you're struggling for a simple way to bypass critical thoughts and access kindness and equanimity toward yourself, try simple mantras like: "I believe in myself. I trust myself. I love and accept myself no matter what. I gift myself with kindness and compassion."

> *There'll only be just ONE of ME*
> *To show what I can do—*
> *And you should likewise feel very proud,*
> *There's only ONE of YOU.*
> *-from "One and Only You" by James T. Moore*[4]

External Judgments

Our critical minds are never content to stop with ourselves. Self-talk has quite a bit to say about other people as well, in the forms of external judgment or prejudiced thinking. This habit ultimately harms your ability to reach your potential. Wayne Dyer said, "When you judge another, you do not define them. You define yourself." You define yourself as somebody that has *the need to judge*.

The roots of our criticism of others—what they look like, what they're wearing, or how they drink their coffee—lie in human evolution and the parasympathetic nervous system's job of keeping us safe. Faced with a potential threat, we are programmed for a quick calculation, leading to fight or flight. But most of us, on a normal day going about our regular business, are rarely in imminent physical danger. Certainly, our safety is not threatened by a colleague's outfit or the size of another person's Frappuccino. All these unnecessary, habitual judgments of other people do nothing more for us, today, than create a negative inner space.

It's Not About Liking Everybody

Maybe there's that *one* person. You just don't like them. You can't get there or convince yourself otherwise. Fair enough. You're not supposed to

---

[4] https://www.symphonyoflove.net/blog/139/one-and-only-you.html Accessed April, 2020.

like everybody. Listening to your instincts about other people is fine. God gave us the gift of natural preferences, certain affinities for some people but not others. Chances are good you can benefit tremendously from learning to listen to your gut more than to your learned people-pleasing habits.

The discipline of being able to suspend judgment isn't about liking everybody. It's about being deliberately present in your thoughts as opposed to allowing the inner dialogue to constantly run amok. Most of us have terrible training and programming in this area. From the way family units interact with love and kindness (or not) to all of the media we've consumed (too often a cadence of disrespectful, derogatory barbs manufactured for a laugh), we don't have many models of reliable equanimity toward self and others.

And that's too bad.

Because the fact remains that you cannot do anything without adequate bandwidth for productivity and hustle toward your short-, mid- and long-range goals. And while you're busy judging every person you see and making some kind of determination about them, having a dialogue in your head about what is wrong with them or what is right about them, *you are simply not available for higher processes.*

You're busy with all the wrong things. You're way too busy with the internal chatter to move the needle and progress toward your goals. There are nearly 172,000 words in the English language, but studies show that average people use the same 20,000 over and over again. We leave out 90% of the English language! In the same way, as you begin an inventory of your inner dialogue, you will notice that you cycle through the same sets of thoughts over and over.

Cyclical thought patterns lead to repeated behaviors that ultimately limit you. The quality of what you manifest with your hustle is impacted. You're exhausted and you always feel busy—because in your mind, you are! You're completely busy every second of the day, talking to yourself, judging others, or comparing yourself to them.

Prodro Pro Tip: Take a snapshot of your life. For a day or so, jot down what you hear in your self-talk, without judging or changing what you hear. Then, make a mental note to interrupt this torrent. Suspend the cadence of judgments toward yourself and others who are not imposing a physical threat to you. You'll discover new time, increased bandwidth, and the positive energy you need to light and feed your fire.

Returning to Resilience

All mindset work is ultimately in service of your resilience. I saved this concept for last in this chapter because I love the word and the concept of resilience. Yet I find its common definition sorely lacking. According to the dictionary, resilience is "the ability to handle adversity, tragedy, and bounce back to the original state."

What truly matters to me, however, is *evolutionary resilience.*

Your goal is not to bounce back to how you were before, but to evolve into the *next* iteration of yourself, toward your higher self and your God-given potential. Even conventional resilience after facing adversity and tragedy is logically flawed because we emerge fundamentally changed from these experiences.

Don't buy into what is being marketed currently as "grit," or the ability to dig in, handle things, and get your life back. Go over hills, reinvent yourself. Find a new, better normal! In this life, we have an incredible opportunity given to us through self-awareness and free will to become observers, to evaluate our evolutionary resilience and develop new and stronger muscles that will carry us through and to the *next* challenge.

For those of you who are willing to take a big leap, consider where your resilience muscles come from, without judgment. This is, again, an opportunity for self-inquiry and deeper self-knowledge, which lead to more powerful progress toward excellence.

- Where did you learn those coping skills?
- Did the experience include getting stuck, or getting revenge?
- Was there a lot of fear, or was it something that made you feel stronger?
- Were there clear distinctions between black or white, right or wrong?

We all learn to cope partially by nature and partially by nurture. Just as we are born with certain cognitive abilities that can be developed over time, we each have an inborn and a learned capacity for resilience. You observe the ways your closest family and friends handled adversity, and you learned something.

Life will continue to send challenges your way. You have the power to choose what to mimic or mirror, and how you want to evolve. The resilience muscles you develop will carry you through those challenges, on to the next stage of growth.

Prodro Pro Tip: Take a moment to do a personal inventory of three things that have happened to you that you didn't expect. Think of things that were out of the blue, tragic, offered adversity. Next to each one, make a note of how you handled them. Did you bounce back or move forward?

CHAPTER 5 GUIDED JOURNALING EXERCISE

1. **My definition of forgiveness is:**

2. **I want to/don't want to forgive because:**

3. **I need to forgive myself and/or others for:**

The Big Idea: Forgiveness is a gift to yourself. It is not permission to be mistreated by yourself or others. Instead, forgiveness is a cathartic release of toxicity that blocks your forward progress. You deserve to be free.

CHAPTER 6

THE FOURTH INFLUENCE: CHOICES

Stop looking for happiness and start looking for meaning.
-from The OPA Way by Alex Pattakos and Elaine Dundon

Closely related to a success-oriented mindset are the body of habits—the choices—you actually exercise each day. How you show up in the world matters. All of your habits rely on your baseline: how you claim your place in the world, and how you navigate your day. Everybody walks out the front door and projects something, whether they know it or not. They project their family history, the nature of their self-talk, their capacity for forgiveness or resilience, and what they're focusing on. The balance between hustle and flow is palpable in our mindset and in our habits.

Will you be in flow or kick ass today?

Can you choose both?

Baseline Presence

Your presence is all wrapped up into a ball of energy that travels around you everywhere you go, and can be immediately felt by others. We might see its effects reflected in how you carry yourself and interact with others. Your baseline presence has a tremendous impact on your effectiveness and the degree to which you can successfully pursue your goals.

Let's walk through a typical day. Look for the ways that balanced hustle and flow are present. Look for the ways your baseline presence *makes* or *allows* things to happen and supports or detracts from your short-, medium-, and long-term goals.

It's morning. You have all sorts of interactions with your family. Things are going well enough, and when you need to, you're using micro-forgiveness strategies to handle rejection and conflict. A micro-forgiveness strategy is a 30-second reset plan. It is something that grounds you, addresses the issue head on, and gives you permission to move on without residual emotional drag. One of mine is that when I perceive rejection or a slight in the conversation, I interrupt by saying, "That is interesting." Then, I may ask for a moment to run to the restroom or to get a better reception on the call.

If I experience a conflict on the road, I may pull off for a quick cup of coffee. These strategies put me back in control and change the dynamic of the moment. They have come to serve me well. I rely on my intuition of when I am going down a bad emotional path, and use micro-forgiveness strategies to provide me relief to take control back. It reminds me of the lane assist in my new VW Atlas. Whenever I veer out of my lane, it guides me back.

Let's return to our day: You're on the court, course correcting all the while, and you have a beautiful morning with your family. You've finished your wellness routine, your meditation or meaningfulness practice, and some time management planning. So far, so good.

You are ready to embark on the day. You get in the car and the first thing you encounter is traffic. It is the first opportunity to practice and model your baseline presence. It will answer the question:

Who am I in the universe and how do I claim my space?

One approach is to become an aggressive driver—weaving through traffic in the certainty that where you're going is more important. Everybody else is simply in your way. Or, are you calm and confident? Are you proactive? Are you careful and methodical, a defensive driver?

Perhaps you are baselined in fear; you've been in car accidents and are now perpetually on the lookout for someone getting in your way or hitting you.

No matter where you began, where are you now in the balance of hustle and flow? Are you more on one side than the other? This is life's challenge and opportunity. Did you allot enough time so that you don't have to stress about an extra five minutes or missing a light? What if somebody is in the way, do you go around? Do you sit back and wait until the car moves out of the way? Do honk loudly or rage against injustice?

Now you go for gas, and the pump doesn't work. A sign tells you to go inside. Do you get frustrated and drive somewhere else instead of taking the 30 seconds to walk inside? (I'm guilty of this!) If, unlike me, you go inside to pay, do you stop for a coffee also? How do you interact with the store clerk? There is so much here that reveals your ability to balance hustle and flow.

Your baseline presence, your standing in life, and all of your achievements and successes will be reflected in your ability to navigate traffic, wait in line, and interact with the person taking money for gas. Your presence will be obvious in your level of confidence, your consideration of others, and your general approach to the challenges of real life.

This does not make one person or one approach right or wrong. But you must know where you reside so you can make intentional choices. There are defensive drivers and then there are people in the flow. There are aggressive drivers and there are proactive people. Look for Goldilocks: life is going to be more difficult lived at either end of the spectrum.

Back to the car, now you're in traffic. Nearly to your office, then into the parking lot. By now, where are you on the spectrum between hustle and flow? Are you going to race into that parking spot that someone else was waiting for? Will you circle endlessly, looking for one but never being assertive enough to claim yours? Do you take the furthest spot a quarter-mile away either because walking is easier than potential conflict over limited spots, or in mindful gratitude for your two healthy legs? There's so much opportunity for self-awareness in something as simple as a parking spot.

Hustle, Flow, and Other People

You arrive at your office, and your interaction with the very first person you see is significant. Perhaps it's with a receptionist, an intern, or your boss. Do you look them in the eye and say hello? If you're looking at your feet or your phone, you nonverbally communicate that what you're doing is more important than the human being in front of you. Correctly or not, others interpret your interrupted gaze as a message that you don't have the time, desire, or energy to acknowledge and interact with them.

This interaction is likely to last for only a split second, so make eye contact, wave, break yourself away from technology, and make a decision that your baseline presence is willing to share a millisecond that will never exist again. In doing so, you'll send a positive ripple into the universe. It means a lot, whether you are the CEO, an entry-level employee, or the building janitor.

As you walk through your building, you're going to encounter many other people. All human beings have an inherent desire to be acknowledged. If you're very busy and must walk and email at the same time, do what's needed. But there's no reason not to smile and make eye contact in an elevator. Kindness costs you nothing and earns you everything.

Notice your baseline level of confidence. On the spectrum of being a positive influence versus a negative presence, where are you in terms of consideration, respectfulness, and being present in the moment? Do you push your agenda onto others? Do you have a mean or edgy streak when you're under pressure? Are you the one rejecting those around you in overt or subtle ways?

Your Energy Ripples Outward at All Times

The next place to look for your baseline orientation to life is how you manage and direct your energy at work. Do you go directly to the coffee pot? Do you allow a little bit of chitchat and then keep your head down for the rest of the day? Do you join in the conversation with a big group meeting?

If your work demands a high-energy hustle, where is the balance? The way to achieve and accomplish all of your goals may require you to be *more* present and take your foot off the accelerator. In other words, you may need to cultivate flow for sustainability.

"I've got strategies for that," you think—and in so doing, resourcefulness becomes your new standing in life, your new baseline. See how this works?

You go through the same cycle each day. As you begin to see your projections, your varying levels of confidence, the quality of your self-talk, everything that we've discussed to this point, it all culminates in your baseline presence, your manifestation of life.

At all times, in all moments, you are choosing what energy ripples will you send out into the universe. Will your ripples be self-absorbed and short-sighted? Will your energy ripples be made of strength, kindness, or vulnerability? You decide.

For most of us, it will be a combination. Finding the right balance between hustle and flow will give you the most fulfilling baseline presence and the most power in carving out your legacy in the world.

Agendas, Time Management, and Accountability

What is the one thing we all share, no matter how much money we have, where we live, or what language we speak? It's the only thing we can never get more of.

It's *time;* how you spend your one and precious life.

This is a topic near and dear to my work with Entrepreneurs and Executives around the world as the critical importance of time management *cannot* be overestimated. It is your most precious, limited, finite, non-refundable resource. Why wouldn't you want to make the best use of it?

Prodro Pro Tip: Get a grip on how much time you are spending in proportion to how important the tasks you are accomplishing actually are to your bigger goals.

First, get real about wasted time. And by this I do *not* mean time spent in ultimately constructive, relaxed flow states are ever wasted. On the contrary, it is in the silence that you hear the voice of God. Here, I am talking about numbing behaviors like social media scrolling. It's human nature to be attracted to things that make us feel good. Dopamine is a hormone released when we spend time in pleasurable ways, and there is now research documenting all of the dopamine hits we get with each social media engagement we receive. No wonder so many people are falling into screen addiction, compulsive digital behaviors, and hiding from their life behind electronics.

Even though we are the most connected we've ever been to one another, in many ways, we are the *least authentically connected* we've ever been. You can live your life with that cyber sense of connection without actually talking to other humans.

In 2009, 89 males and 98 females over the age of 80 from Ikaria Island, Greece, were voluntarily enrolled in a study about longevity, daily habits, psychological characteristics, and lifestyle. The percentage of people over 90 in Ikaria was much higher than the European population average. The majority of the oldest participants reported daily physical activities, healthy eating habits, avoidance of smoking, frequent socializing, mid-day naps, and extremely low rates of depression.[5]

Social media? Not on the list!

Your biggest source of fruitlessly spent time is likely in your hand or your pocket right now. A source of previously-unimaginable knowledge, information, and connection also consume hours and hours of the day. At work, we are largely distracted, less productive, less engaged, and less happy. Our phones and other devices are addictive and their content is specifically curated to capture your attention and take you down a rabbit hole of content. You don't want to feel like you are on Mr. Toad's Wild Ride at Disney. And yet often, you are.

Of course, the online social landscape is not all negative. For many small businesses, social media is a non-negotiable part of the business environment; it's where they gain leads and create genuine connections with people. We can share information and resources in response to loss and tragedy like never before, ultimately helping one another in wider ways than ever before. We reconnect and rekindle old friendships, find family members and celebrate friends' successes.

But be aware of all the time you *could* be spending pursuing your goals and creating meaning while being an observer of other people's lives. The habit of churning out endless posts that only make you look good is *not* being productive unless your career goals specifically and intentionally benefit from having a curated public persona.

No one wants to talk about it, but I've observed a polarizing phenomenon over the last decade in which people are moving to the extremes with what they share. Either they are showing the very best parts

---

[5] https://www.ncbi.nlm.nih.gov/pmc/articles/PMC3051199/ Accessed April, 2020.

of their life, bragging, or posting only about their own achievements (or those of their children) OR they've moved to the other extreme, using platforms as a vent for victimhood, resentment, and abject negativity. In the current divisive political climate, digital media is particularly addictive.

You need a plan for managing it and using it to your advantage, rather than allowing it to use you. Create a discipline to abide by and a metric to know when you've veered off track. This is the number key to meeting your daily goals.

A man in his twenties recently shared something on LinkedIn about his morning routine: immediately after waking, he would read through each one of his social channels. Then, he would start all over again, going back through and liking/commenting/posting on other people's posts and creating his own throughout the day. In his post, he talked about stepping away from that habit. In its place, he created a freedom time management plan for himself wherein he set aside a half hour at the start of each day:

- He listed the things he was grateful for.
- He listed three things that needed to happen that day, and then three other things that he could do to continue working towards a long-term goal.
- Finally, he listed three things that he could do that day to contribute to others, a core value of his.

This is a fine example of an integrated, human approach. He was driven to be productive, meet his immediate goals, and progress on his larger ones, and give back. I'm sure he still uses social media. But he uses it as a tool, not a director. Thus, it facilitated his plan for the day and for his life. It no longer *ran* his life.

How might *you* create a sustainable and effective time management plan for yourself? Let's talk about some possible solutions.

Planners

In the days of coaching business executives on time management, we used paper books similar to the Franklin Covey planner. Whether you choose the analog route or a digital calendar on your phone and computer, there are two critical points: I recommend having only one calendar. Maximum, one calendar and one planner, if they are mutually exclusive.

One of Stephen Covey's greatest contributions is his suggestion to break down your daily goals according to your roles: whether at work, as a parent or member of a family, a student, etc. Your calendar needs to reflect that you are a whole person and need a holistic view of your life, personally and professionally. Otherwise, it won't work. When your roles and integrity align with your actions, you are balancing hustle and flow.

Start Your Day Right

I recommend starting your day in the flow. Begin with your exercise routine or something for your physical health and wellness. Then begin a short morning meditation, either silently or with an audio recording. Make a short gratitude list. After this, begin planning for your day. Skip social media and launch into your routine: perhaps check email and respond accordingly.

Email

For business people, email is often the number one consideration for successful time management and freedom. Put your morning's first emails into several categories by immediate importance to less urgent. (There may be tools to aid you in this: Google email currently offers a reminder function when you have not answered an important email.) Then research, respond, and archive.

Rather than spending one of every five minutes on your phone each day, develop a discipline of checking email in larger chunks (unless you are involved in something quite urgent). Check only once in the morning, once in the afternoon, and then at the end of the day. You will improve your productivity 100 percent.

Are you feeling resistance to this idea? Many people do.

When email is on your handheld device, it is easy to fall into a mindset that you must take immediate action on things. It's a pervasive challenge for so many of us. There is such an incredible *volume* of information, intake emails, text messages, direct messages, and phone calls coming in that I went through a phase of answering everything immediately. I could not stand the prospect of having everything backing up into impossibly daunting piles. But even that became impossible. I learned that for 90 percent of the people reaching out to me, it's completely appropriate to leave a few hours or more in between response times.

Be mindful of when you seek a dopamine (the feel-good chemical) boost by checking email or social notifications. We all know that it is a gamble because we might find something stressful, rather than supportive. This compulsive "checking" behavior is equivalent to screaming "someone notice me!" In the balance, we are working toward building good feelings coming from within you instead of from external sources.

Managing External Interruptions

Between getting a handle on social media and email's domination of your day, you will create a meaningful transformation in your efficiency, productivity, and wellness. Next, turn your attention to other interruptions and time wasters.

What is distracting you on a regular basis? At your work, it could be people that come to your desk to interrupt and ask questions. If you work from home, maybe it's the dog, or UPS knocking at the door, or the temptation to tackle the laundry pile instead of tackling the nagging work project.

Some interruptions are just the result of life. There's no one to blame. But if you are prone to distraction, track how many interruptions you have and when you tap into your deeply focused creative time. Create environments or blocks of time in places where you're sequestered, somewhere you can actually escape from those distractions. You might not even realize that distraction is happening over and over again. You may not consider how much you can do to actually control your time in a more meaningful way.

Prodro Pro Tip: For the next week, make a mental note of all the ways and times that you lose productivity to outside distractions.

Just Three Things

Next is learning the discipline of prioritization. When I say *the three things that must get done*, you would be surprised how many people have trouble describing what must be done. It's easy to have a never-ending to do list. But taking a moment to identify *what's most important now* will help you move mountains. And let's be honest, that long list overwhelms you because everybody has way too much to do.

One thing shared by the most productive people is the way they stick to their priorities. While they're at work on one of their three top things, and something inevitably pops into their head or an email generates a different to-do, they take that task or information, and place it on the calendar exactly where it should be on the date they will look at it again. Then, they return to the job at hand. Adapting this one habit is going to make you extremely productive.

"Must happen" versus "should happen" will help create your personal roadmap for success.

How I Manage It

I have three children. I'm single. I run several businesses. I'm a public speaker and an author. People often ask me how I get it all done. The answer? A foundation of time management discipline and habits has afforded me the opportunity to focus on the most important things. I do not have a 10-page to-do list because when a task arises, it is placed on my calendar for when I need to look at it next. I never have stress and nagging anxiety, or worry that I'm forgetting something.

It's simple but not easy, and it's a skill developed over time. Remember, the whole purpose of time management is to alleviate stress—to afford you the opportunity to live in the balance between hustle and flow.

Time Management in Action

Let's say I'm driving and suddenly remember I received an inquiry from the US Patent & Trademark Office in the mail. It had a deadline on it by when I had to respond. Uh oh. Did I address that trademark question already? Did I miss the date? It should have been placed on the calendar with a date and time somewhere so I wouldn't miss it.

When I get where I'm going, I open my planner, email, or project management software. Did I respond already? No. Is it on the calendar? I did a search for USPTO. Yes, there it was, scheduled for next Thursday; the deadline is in two weeks. Whew.

Even though the question popped into my head and nagged at me, I've got peace. I know it will get done because I've set aside time for it next Thursday. If I had the feeling that I wanted to get it off my mind and off my list, great, I'd move it to today and change the calendar accordingly. I gave myself a week's leeway before the deadline so that if it got put off next Thursday, or if I was sick, or I had to fly out of town, or had an emergent opportunity, I would still have the time to take care of it.

Remember, the whole reason for these systems is to *alleviate* stress.

If you're an expert in time management, whenever something comes at you or flies through your head, put it on the calendar on the date you are going to execute that task. If life gets in the way, as it sometimes does, and the task doesn't get that done that day, move it to the next day. *Never place it on the day before it's due.* Over time, you will learn to adapt this process with ease and flow according to your needs, your productivity, and the size of your workload.

Prodro Pro Tip: For the next week, make a mental note of all the ways and times that you lose productivity to outside distractions.

Snail Mail and Bills

Archaic as it may be, when you receive mail that generates the need for an action, handle it in much the same fashion as you handle your email. Keep a file on your desk of open items. If you touch it once, it either gets filed away or it gets put in an active inbox and placed on your calendar. Within your open items file, keep only short-term items for up to one month. Everything else needs a more permanent home, whether hard copy or digital. Consider apps that take photos of documents and attach them as PDFs to your calendar or inbox. Then file away the piece of paper and stay on track as the mail comes in.

The number one stress people have in managing their finances, other than a shortage of funds, is keeping track of when everything is due. No one wants to part with their money before it's due, but we also endure great stress with the constant nagging of the question of what's due when. Whether you are more comfortable with paper bills and checks or everything electronic, I certainly recommend you have a plan for how you handle your personal and professional finances that allows you to relax, knowing it's taken care of. Your first thought in the morning should not be, "Uh oh, did I pay my American Express?" or "I'm not sure that I paid the water bill this month."

Haphazard receipts all over the desk is *not* a plan. Having all of these nagging reminders sit there creates stress and will interfere with your ability to reach your higher goals. You'll only be able to achieve a state of flow with excellent time management. When all of these stress triggers don't come up because you're confident with the plan you have in place, you can rest easy knowing that you have placed the task where it needs to go.

This only happens if you bring it to life by working your plan every day.

Let's review: you wake up. It's Tuesday. You're *not* going to go on social media first thing. Instead, you begin your wellness routine, leaving you feeling energized and clear. Meditate. Read the Bible. Exercise. Watch a video featuring Richard Branson, Oprah, or Gary Zukav.

Then, begin your own personal daily plan chunk by chunk: review email in the beginning, middle, and end of the day. If social media is an important part of your work or you have a productive reason to visit and post on these platforms, allot a maximum of three visits a day per channel: during the morning, afternoon, and evening. Make sure it's a *discipline*.

If you need to immediately respond to a message as you make your way through the day, leave it open on your desktop. Work on the top three items that must be completed in the different categories—the items that you previously placed on your calendar for that day. Execute those first. If you do not finish them, move the leftover tasks to the day that you're going to actually do them. The next morning when you begin, review the prior day. Be sure every incomplete task has been placed on your calendar. Hold yourself accountable.

Do this and you will dramatically increase your discipline, happiness, and time management. You'll have less stress and a more focused, intentional, and productive life. You will also achieve so many more of your immediate, midterm, and long-range goals.

Prodro Pro Tip: Whatever method you find works for your discipline design, I highly recommend you spend the first 30 minutes of every day in meditation, meaningfulness, gratitude, and planning. This is about *quality* of life, not only the *quantity* of your accomplishments.

CHAPTER 6 GUIDED JOURNALING EXERCISE

1. **Who am I in the universe and how do I claim my space (baseline presence of the way I am)?**

2. **Three words I use to describe myself:** (enduring personality characteristics like happy, angry, or outgoing)

3. **After interacting with me, how do I typically leave others feeling at work? In my personal life?**

The Big Idea: Freedom from nagging thoughts comes from being organized and managing your time. This discipline can be equally applied to flow in scheduling time to sit with your actions and do nothing. The balance between hustle and flow is achieved in understanding their truly complementary nature.

CHAPTER 7

THE FIFTH INFLUENCE: PASSION

It is not the critic who counts; not the man who points out how the strong man stumbles, or where the doer of deeds could have done them better. The credit belongs to the man who is actually in the arena. ~Theodore Roosevelt

The word "passion" evokes many emotions and meanings. In Greek, we use the word *Meraki*. Meraki is to do something with passion, with absolute devotion and unfettered attention. Putting your soul into anything is the essence of Meraki Passion; there is a little bit of yourself in any work, task, expression or artistic endeavor.

There is also the obvious reference to love when most of us think about professional passion, as in "Love What You Do." The Greeks offer four words for love with different nuances:

1) Storgi - Love of family
2) Eros - Romantic love
3) Philia - Love between friends
4) Agape - Unconditional love and love of God

The passion we will discuss here relates to passion of the true self or true gift passion. The easiest way to relate to this is to ask yourself what you would be doing with your days if there was no such thing as money. What do you do that makes time seem to melt away or changes your perception of time even existing?

For some of us, it helps to adjust the question: our passion is the secret answer to what *we would do if we knew we could not fail*. Passion for a vocation, a path, an expression of self, a life calling comes from deep within the soul. Passion cannot be given to you; rather it is a gift your Creator has given you that you have a lifetime to unwrap.

The holy grail of existence, as Gary Zukov shares in his bestselling book *Seat of the Soul*, is "when the personality comes fully to serve the energy of its soul, that is authentic empowerment."

Unwrapping Your Gifts

Why is it that some people succeed in finding and expressing their passion very early on with precision and strength? There is no easy answer to this question, but taking a moment to reflect on the patterns of your life may reveal some insight into what to do next, how to get started, where to level up, or how to inspire others. Sometimes it takes others to point out the obvious or give you permission to unwrap your passion. Just because this is divine does not mean you will be perfect or even good at it. But I encourage you to dig deep and examine your passion and how much you are honoring it or bringing it to life in this world.

When I was in high school, I was a Student Council Officer each year. In my senior year, it earned me the honor of making the morning announcements over the intercom. With pride and sheer happiness, I grabbed the microphone each morning to read off the lunch menu (I added my own humorous twist and it must have been memorable because one of my teachers posted about it on Facebook this year, decades later). I also announced club meetings and special events. Doing this each day forged my connection to the entire student body. No surprise, communication is my passion.

In addition, I was in the Drama Club (are you shocked?), the School Lunch Menu Planning Committee (when I am all in, there are few boundaries) and more. It made my days amazing. My normal teenage angst was definitely mitigated by expressing my passion—by being so involved. Not everyone has an obvious passion like mine for public speaking, writing, and connecting with large groups and communities.

The *journey* to discovery can be fulfilling. My best friend says she doesn't know hers yet (she is 50) but has done amazing, meaningful work along the way all the while striving for the excellence we discussed in Chapter One. She is still unwrapping her passion.

The true gift of self-awareness is part of the hustle and flow. Let the truth be revealed and success leaves clues. The famous psychiatrist Carl Jung said, "Until you make the unconscious conscious, it will direct your life and you will call it fate." This journey takes a balance between hustle and flow, knowing when to let things happen and when to make them happen, creates a sought-after quiet strength.

Moments of Clarity

Did you ever have a moment or two that felt so right you didn't want it to end? They depict this in movies by making time stand still or slowing it down. They punctuate it with dramatic music. When you experience this kind of significant moment, it is an indication that your energy is vibrating at the best frequency. Notice who is around you. These moments often require the presence of like-minded individuals or at least the absence of anyone creating static or opposing you.

Here are a few of mine from points across my life:

1. Volunteering to run the school store
2. Running for student council
3. Making the morning announcements
4. Being selected as a delegate to meet with the Undersecretary of State in college
5. Presenting to groups to get them to do fundraising for the Multiple Sclerosis Society
6. Leading the "Macarena" at a National Sales Conference
7. Turning on the microphone when testifying at a Congressional Hearing
8. Being interviewed on a national podcast
9. Encouraging a server to pursue an art career
10. Having a conversation with my three children

In these moments, the world is right. Everyday moments are punctuated with these moments of clarity. What moments do you recall? How have they driven your decisions and gotten you to hustle?

One of my favorite adventures was going up in a hot air balloon in Arizona. Between the noise blasts of the heater, we experienced a peaceful, pure silence floating high above the ground. I felt the same flow when parasailing in Key West. Even though I could see dark shadows of sharks below, it was beautiful in those moments (as long as we didn't slow down to land near them, of course!). People who snorkel or dive leave the world of familiar noise to experience the true majesty of nature. In these moments, our souls are recharged and timeless secrets of passion and purpose can be revealed.

The good news is you can take a deep breath and flow at any moment of a regular day, knowing the steps to the path are appearing as you show faith.

Vibrational Energy

The unseen forces that create and modulate energy are expressed in scientific research and communities. Why do you connect with one person or place, for instance, and feel repelled by others?

Resonance is the natural frequency of synchronistic waves. Natural language mirrors the internal feeling of frequency. Consider the notion of, "I like his vibe," or the song "Good Vibrations" when you think about this idea. Although we may not need to reference the underlying scientific terms, we can all agree that the phenomenon of sensing one another's energy is real.

Where can you find this energy? How can it serve your hustle and flow?

Our gut instincts are amazing gifts when it comes to reading energy. You can find the key and secret to vibrational energy in the way you feel around certain people and places. For example, on a wonderful trip to Arizona recently, I joined my best friend from college, Denise, for a girls' spiritual weekend. On a hike into the scenic mountains surrounding Santa Fe, we came upon two beautiful mountains. We still remember to this day the experience, calling them the "happy mountains."

We both felt blissful in their majesty and happiness in their presence. I can picture them so vividly right now against the perfect blue backdrop of the sky; they appeared a rustic reddish color with the natural texture of healing clay. The two mountains stood together and apart from the others, like ancient friends with secrets. Denise and I kept going deeper on the hike and I remember an overwhelming feeling of emotion. I leaned against a rock to catch my breath and feel whatever it was that was there. How could such a joyous feeling from the "Happy Mountains" now turn to a feeling of sadness? We had moved through this incredible land with its changing vibrations, and I am very sensitive to energy signatures and vibrational energy. We rested a bit and decided to call it a day.

When we returned to the town and did a little research about the location where I felt that profound sense of sadness, we learned it was an ancient Indian burial ground. Sacred ground. Souls rested there and some had even departed right there. Somehow, I had plugged in and felt it all. I was honored and in awe of the power of energy.

Inspirational People

Human connection is divine. Humans will go to great lengths to find it, keep it, and control it. The people in my life have helped me understand passion and encouraged me to go for my dreams. My parents created a home life where we felt heard as children. We knew that our opinions mattered, and our voices were welcomed in every conversation. They were amazing conversationalists and I attribute my success to their influence. We could have differences of opinion without being disrespectful. We shared innovative ideas and thoughts without the risk of being embarrassed or shamed. My parents encouraged our questions at every level to help us dig deeper.

My gratitude for the way they treated us cannot be overstated. It is one of the greatest gifts I have ever received in my life. My place in the world was on firm footing from the earliest age, so I could later unwrap my passion and share it with the world.

My parents died young and my sister and brother, both older, led by example. They continue to offer me support, strength, and unconditional love. If you don't have this naturally, I encourage you to seek friends as your new family to bring out the best in you. Security and sacred trust will be the ultimate foundation to live your best life.

Philotimo! Family, Cousins and Friends

As second-generation Greek Immigrants, my grandmother Theoklia was one of eight siblings. My grandfather George sent for them and they all worked closely to honor the gift of becoming U.S. citizens.

Philotimo is a Greek term that doesn't translate to English. The best way I can describe it is to say it's the love of honor—doing good for the greater good. It's your responsibility and mine. It's a cultural imperative meaning you can be wildly successful but you have an extra inextricable link to humanity to do things that move us forward together.

My father lived out the concept of philotimo when he started his car wash business in New York in the early 1960s. He took on partners, community leaders from diverse ethnic backgrounds, one African-American family, one Puerto Rican family. Their families worked in the business alongside our family, and it was a community. Everybody had a stake in it. Everyone was proud of it. And it was really a shining example of diverse people, of families working together in harmony, at a time when it really wasn't so common.

That's the fabric of who I am.

One side of my family is from Sparta. You know about the Spartan 300, the fiercest warriors ever. The other side of the family is from the center of commerce for the world, Constantinople, which is now Istanbul. In other words, East meets West in my blood, and I feel like it drives me to hustle and invites me to flow.

My Greek heritage is very strong. We have the deepest appreciation for our heritage, but by the same token, adore and love the American opportunities we've received. My life has been driven by deep seated respect for other human beings. It came from both of my parents and my grandparents and it will always form the core of my passion to help others.

Your actions create ripples in the universe beyond anyone's human perception or comprehension. The flow of doing amazing good in the world or serving humanity for the greater good can take many forms. My sister was always a role model to me, especially since my mom died so early. One story really illuminates how fortunate I have been. Themie has four children, and many years ago I remember being in awe of her duty to humanity and selflessness.

She was the Girl Scout troop leader and had a sweet, beautiful girl in her group who, along with her family, became homeless. My sister jumped into her Greek mom energy, into pure hustle action, and collected supplies and goodies to make them more comfortable at the homeless shelter. She was always checking in with the mom to see what she could do to alleviate some of the pain and uncertainty.

The four kids in the family all got lice from the shelter. My sister insisted they come over to her house so she could get the treatment and help them get rid of it. Remember, Themie had four school age children of her own. I thought she was crazy!

"Are you going to expose her whole family to lice to help them?" I asked.

"Of course," she said. "Imagine how they feel. Lice is not serious; if my family gets it, we will treat them, too."

One amazing human, she made a huge difference in their lives and did what she knew was right even though all of us in her family thought she was out of her mind. Fast forward to the future: the young lady who was once in my sister's Girl Scout troop has now graduated from college with honors. She always comes back to visit my sister and credits her with being a fantastic influence, giving her the motivation to achieve her goals. The ripples of Themie's goodness keep going on this earth. I am extremely proud she is my sister.

CHAPTER 7 GUIDED JOURNALING EXERCISE

1. **How does my personality serve the full energy of my soul?**

2. **My passion in life is:**

3. **I lose track of time when I am:**

The Big Idea: We are each a beautiful expression of our Creator, sending out energy in our hustle and flow. The people surrounding us reflect our inner and outer expression and share the journey. Passion is a gift for everyone that can be unwrapped through introspection and gratitude.

CHAPTER 8

THE SIXTH INFLUENCE: SERENDIPITY

How cool is it that the same God that created mountains and oceans and galaxies thought that the world needed one of you too. -Unknown

1. The balance between letting things happen and making things happen is a very delicate one. It is where you live your life.
2. When you know something is beyond what you can comprehend, it is something that will give you insight into the secrets of the

universe. Serendipity is the beautiful balance of how things fit together and when things are meant to be.
3. Faith is the belief in the unseen, unheard, and that which is not physically felt. The pillars of our faith are a sixth sense, strong yet tested, kind yet bold. A personal journey of faith is rudder that keeps you on course to your ultimate destiny and reward.

Zip City

I was born in Manhattan but grew up in Florida. I had traveled back to New York City for business and I was meeting a friend at a restaurant. I got there a bit early and waited in the very crowded bar of a restaurant called Zip City. Directly across from me at the bar sat a gentleman who had a friendly face but didn't look familiar.

I exchanged glances with him and there was kind of a *knowing*. I sensed there was some connection, and smiled. It wasn't a romantic or flirting smile, it was more like an acknowledgement of another human. Soon after, my friend walked in. She came around to me and all of a sudden, the same gentleman came over from the other side of the bar and joined us. It turns out he was her first cousin! I had met him once as a child. I didn't recognize him at all, but somehow knew we were connected before I knew who he actually was.

As we stood in this very busy, crowded, bustling Manhattan bar, we saw another gentleman walk by. I said to my friend, "He looks like my cousin Steve."

My friend's cousin says, "Oh, do you mean Steve M.?"

"My goodness, yes!" I nod. He said he had had lunch with my cousin *that day*.

Not only did we run into my friend's first cousin at this restaurant, he had had lunch with *my* cousin that same day. Yet none of us would have known that if a gentleman didn't walk by who looked like someone in my family. Or, perhaps the universe would have given us another nudge.

My friend's cousin continued his story of how he had lunch for business reasons with my cousin that day. At that lunch, my cousin Steve was accompanied by *yet another cousin* of mine named Ted. (Since I'm Greek, it doesn't really surprise anybody to hear I have cousins and cousins and cousins. Stay with me.)

Ted, whom I hadn't seen in many years, is a very successful architect who was just launching his own business at this time. My friend's cousin had his business card!

To review: we ran into my friend's cousin in a very busy place in Manhattan, and he had business cards from both of *my* cousins.

It reminded me that on my many recent journeys to New York, I hadn't seen my second cousin Steve in some time, and prompted me to reach out to him—to remake an important connection. Ted went on to become a highly influential, wonderful figure in my life after that serendipitous connection. I believe I was meant to reconnect with him. For serendipity to work for you, you have to be open to it. You have to follow those leads. You have to offer your time, energy, and trust.

When things like this happen, there is a greater reason.

It was a great gift from God and the universe to place all the right people in the right places to reconnect me with my cousin.

When have you had an experience like this?

Prodro Pro Tip: Reflect on times in your life when serendipity has helped you personally or professionally. I believe that calling these moments to mind and being open to them helps more of them appear.

Directory Assistance

When I was 12 years old, we lived in Florida. It was in the dinosaur age, meaning there were no cell phones. I was at home and the way to get people's phone numbers was to call directory assistance. It cost a quarter, but my mom occasionally let us do that if we were really stumped. One day I picked the phone up—with permission—and called to get a listing for somebody I wanted to talk to.

I dialed 411.

I heard two strange clicks, and suddenly a man's voice came on the line. This was unusual: when you called directory assistance, you'd get an operator greeting you immediately.

He said, "Hello?"

I said, "Hello?"

He said "Uh, yes, could I have a listing please? For someone in Tarpon Springs, and the last name is Prodromitis."

I almost dropped the phone. *At the exact same time* I was calling directory assistance, one of my brother's friends was calling directory assistance as well. And he was looking for *our* listing. Instead of getting the directory assistant, he was accidentally connected to the Prodromitis residence. I could never even make these details up.

He said again, "I am looking for a listing for Prodromitis."

It felt as if something big was in play because this friend was *supposed* to connect with my brother. He never would have found my brother if he hadn't connected to me. Our phone number was not listed under our complete last name. It was listed under a shortened version, and he would have gotten nowhere, even with an operator's assistance. God and the universe decided to directly connect him, and designed a time and a way. It was a great moment.

I was silent for a moment. To this day, I fully remember that spooky feeling. Cue the *Twilight Zone* music! I responded, "This is the Prodromitis residence." I asked him to hold on and ran and got my brother.

To this day, I feel blessed that I had that experience at 12 years old—to know that anything is possible.

Nothing Can Stop Destiny

Whenever I flew into New York City during my twenties, I would always take a car service located in the neighborhood where my cousin lived. She had a jewelry company in a very artsy area and the car service was located right down the street from her. One day I arrived in town, called the car service, and discovered they had no cars available.

Before the internet we only had the phone book, so I opened it up and went down the pages to look for a car service in New York City. I started at the top with the A's. The first one I called just rang and rang. Nobody answered. Then I went to the second one. Someone picked up and then left me on hold. When they returned, they were very abrupt and rude, so I hung up and I went to the third one, which was called Allstate. They were very helpful, so I reserved a car.

The Balance Between Hustle & Flow

The operator taking the reservation asked "Okay, what is your last name?" I started to spell it: P R O D R O M I T I S.

She said, "That's my boss's last name."

I said, "Really? What's his first name?"

"He goes by Dennis, but his real first name is longer. It's a Greek name."

I said, "Well, that's amazing, because that's my brother's name."

It turns out her boss was my first cousin! A long-lost first cousin, in fact, because years before, his father died and his mother moved to a different area. We had completely lost touch, which is unheard of in a close big Greek family. But we had no idea where she was, and before the internet you couldn't just find people, especially if they changed their name, or went by a different last name.

So here he was, my very first cousin with the very same name.

It's uncanny, the extraordinary sequence of events that God and the universe had to align for me in order to meet Dennis. All because my traditional car service wasn't available. My cousin ended up picking me up. He later reconnected with our whole family, visiting Florida to meet us and spend time with us. And praise God that he did, because he died young, about 10 years after we were reunited. But we got the chance to rekindle our family relationship and friendship. It was all arranged by serendipity and in my world, GOD.

CASE STUDY: *I had a successful friend, we'll call her Jessica, who had a very high-level position with the federal government. She held an advanced degree and was doing well enough, but could not stand her work environment. She felt like she was being held back by her superiors. Her bosses were not promoting her, and she feared they didn't have her best interest at heart.*

After speaking with Jessica about how to transition or change careers, we spoke about that magical place in between letting it happen and making it happen. I suggested she go out on a limb and to create something totally new. Go to the place of hustle and really stir something up, create something out of nothing. Then leave it alone and see what develops.

There was another field Jessica wanted to work in: the role of art in business. I suggested that since she had fantastic writing skills, she could write an article on the topic she was interested in. That could open up the door. That is the hustle part—she would reach out to connections to help her identify great candidates to interview for the piece she was writing, and then learn about what they're doing in that field.

The idea I offered Jessica that day is the same one I am offering you: put it out there. Create something from nothing. Stake a claim that you are going to create value.

So, Jess wrote a piece communicating her insights about what was important in her business. And then she let it go from there. Since this was an area of passion for my friend, she was able to tell a compelling story. When she did that, I was able to contact some people and make introductions. There were other people she knew she could reach out to as well. I told her, "You've got to make a decision. You've got to hustle and make a decision. Just pick a week, and then whoever can be interviewed that week in that new town will come through."

One of the companies my friend was most interested in came through. They contacted her. This wasn't surprising to me at all. Once she took control and hustled for a space in which she could create something new, all the pieces started to fall in place.

She decided to move to another state and continue working in law, but she was forever changed by the experience, and by the idea that hustle and flow can help you create any path you desire. It was in a conversation with her that the first idea for this book was born. I said, "This is the balance between hustle and flow." And she got this great look on her face and said, "That is the title of your book." Thank you, Jess!

This is the balance of the flow in action. You reach out to people, and do your due diligence. Then, you let in the flow, trusting that those who respond are the ones who bring serendipity along with them. The connections that are meant to be will happen. They are supposed to be in your life; supposed to be a part of this process.

None of it happens with only one side or the other, because *the magic is in the balance.* If you just sit back and let things happen, there's not enough energy to move anything forward. Push and force relentlessly, you'll burn through all of your energy and your luck before you reach the goal.

Because that's how serendipity works. It is available and unlimited for now today and every day.

CHAPTER 8 GUIDED JOURNALING EXERCISE

1. **My beliefs about serendipity are:**

2. **The strangest coincidence I have ever experienced is:**

3. **I have felt serendipity or connections I cannot explain on these occasions:**

The Big Idea: Serendipity can be called by many names. It is more of a feeling than an event. When you sense that a divine appointment or a connection needs to be made, sit back and enjoy the ride. It is a reminder of the infinite wisdom that connects us all to Source.

PART III

THE BIG QUESTIONS

CHAPTER 9

THE FIRST QUESTION: WHAT DO I REALLY WANT?

Exponential growth comes from aligning your goals with your integrity.
Theo Prodromitis

Personal Identity: Who Are *You*?

Your personal story is important because it helps other people connect and understand how you might play a role in their lives. It is quickly communicated through your personal identity and the first three things you say about yourself. Wise people know this and use it to their advantage.

In addition, *the stories you tell* and *the way you describe yourself* in a narrative reflect whether you are a person who lives in the past or in the future. The adjectives you choose reveal whether you talk about *what is*, your vision for *what is becoming*, and what *you are evolving to do*.

It is critical that the story you tell yourself (to yourself and to the world) be a story that speaks concisely to your values and your mission in life. Arriving at this clarity in language is not easy, but it conveys immense power and opens doors you might never anticipate.

Prodro Pro Tip: Ask: What are the first three words you use to describe yourself? Mine are: Greek, Mom, Entrepreneur.

You Can Never Get Enough of What You *Don't* Want

What you focus on expands in the balance between hustle and flow. This is a great opportunity for powerful manifestation—and a bit of a warning about the importance of a clear and articulate mindset that speaks in the affirmative. Most of the classic manifestation book *The Secret* focuses on gaining material wealth. It was wildly successful because people want to know how to manifest the things they want.

But as Wayne Dyer pointed out, "You can never get enough of what you don't want." And too many people make the devastating mistake of prioritizing what they don't want, rather than what they do want.

I'll back up a bit. Whatever receives attention sets in motion a set of circumstances through which the universe conspires with you to bring forward a beautiful creation process. What you focus on expands. It's a universal law to me that gets proven every day. But the universe is deaf to the words "don't," "doesn't," and "isn't." If you say, "I don't want debt, I hate my debt, debt doesn't serve me," all that expands is debt.

Perhaps it is rooted in the positive nature of creation. The subject combined with emotion continues to manifest it. Even if the emotion is negative, it is the strength of the visualization, certainty, and topic. Add to that the constant repetition.

Mother Teresa embodied this truth. She understood the power of stating things in the positive and not trying to negate war. In her book, No Greater Love she shares her ageless wisdom about only speaking of peace.

You say: "I don't want a man who is an alcoholic or a boss who is a jerk."

The Universe hears: "I want a man who is an alcoholic and a boss who is a jerk."

You say: "I only want to date men who don't smoke."

Guess what the Universe hears? Now you've met nine terrific people in a row—who all smoke. It's the (sometimes frustrating) elegant simplicity of a universal law in action.

If you're feeling skeptical, take a moment to actively suspend your disbelief for just a moment. Haven't there been times that the clearer you get about what you *don't* want, the more it seems to show up on your doorstep? Disbelievers chalk up this phenomenon to accidents, flukes, or bad luck. But if you want to access the full power of hustle and flow, you need to be more specific and clearer in articulating what you *do* want than what you *don't* want.

Write it down.

Then hustle a bit; take appropriate action, make connections, bring it forward.

Imagine you're shopping for a car and deciding between Hondas and BMWs. Before, you never noticed either of them much, but suddenly everywhere you go, they fill the road! It's not that they didn't exist before; they're appearing to you now because you're shopping for them. Your attention is on those cars, and they appear. This is just a classic chicken and the egg thing, some people argue. Are you bringing the cars forth *because* you're focusing on them now, or are you just noticing them now that you're paying attention?

In the balance between hustle and flow, it simply doesn't matter.

What really matters is that you recognize the process by which you can get more of what you want: by paying attention to what you desire. When you begin to notice this fact at play in your life, you can never not see it again.

I am extremely passionate about female entrepreneurs and building each other up. I am aware of income inequality but focus on recognition of qualifications and accomplishments. The International Women's Day 2020 slogan "each for equal" did not resonate with me. I know I will get a lot of push back on this, but it is the absolute truth. In my heart, I support women's empowerment. I bring it to life by focusing on removing all barriers to being paid and recognized for what we earn, deserve, and accomplish.

However, men are not the benchmark to be measured against. Our own potential is the measurement.

Women can do anything and everything, and we do. I focus on each human's potential and harnessing the strength in 51% of the population begins with recognizing other women. Then, I see the synergy of potential being made real and not beginning behind the premise of being equal to anything. I want to see women compensated for our accomplishments and potential.

When I set out to reach a broader audience with my "Light Your Fire" focus on personal potential, I was recognized with more opportunities than you can imagine, from testifying in Congress, to being a founding member of the Zuckerberg Institute, to co-authoring a book with Jack Canfield to winning an Enterprising Women of the Year Award.

On Vulnerability & Authenticity

Just as your fulfillment depends on balancing hustle and flow, your happiness in life depends on balancing your strength and vulnerability. While these concepts may sound ethereal, they are already tangibly integrated into every second of your life.

There are conflicting messages today about the value of vulnerability and authenticity and the opposing pressure to *fake it 'til you make it:* to make everything look good and the positive results will follow.

Just as with everything else we have discussed we walk a fine line in search of a productive balance. This is yet another dichotomy that requires us to course-correct and learn as we go.

As you are approaching your goals and your highest aspirations in life, fears will come up. There's no way around it. The fear of not achieving what you set out to do. The fear of rejection, the fear of loss, the fear of loss of income. The fear of outgrowing your family and friends.

Yes, there's a certain vulnerability in the balance between hustle and flow, particularly relating to business and your standing in the world. It can be a challenge to maintain your strength while making decisions about how much to share about your fears, or any of the other difficulties that would give people an insight into your vulnerability, into a real part of you.

We all have a human need to be seen for who we truly are. It may benefit you to share a moment of vulnerability with a coworker, showing them that everything is not perfect. You may need their opinion or advice on a sensitive topic. But following that conversation up with a personal text message or a deeper dive to intimacy beyond business—that's oversharing. Hustle to connect and let the true connection flow without overdoing it.

Yes, everyone must determine their own comfort level and personal boundaries according to their goals.

For some, it's part of their personal brand to disclose details of a divorce, or their financial problems, or their challenges with their children. Some are open about their business challenges or their self-doubt. There's no objectively right or wrong answer about whether to share this kind of personal information.

But always consider *whether you're getting the results that you want* based on the amount of vulnerability that you share. If your goals are to refine, improve, or increase your productivity or your leadership abilities, are you being authentic and vulnerable—or are you oversharing?

Traditionally, men in high executive positions rank lower on sharing and vulnerability. They typically share fewer personal stories and vulnerabilities when they're faced with a difficult decision. Powerful women in leadership positions often have greater facility with balancing the powerful and the personal.

As an example of someone who effectively demonstrates this balance, consider Richard Branson. He often shares his authenticity, but everybody knows he's still in control. He's a leader who can out-hustle anybody. Yet from day one, well before he was a billionaire, he served others and increased his vulnerability by having mental health and counseling hotlines as part of his business model. To this day, he publicly honors nature, the earth, and his personal passion for environmentalism.

This is the balance between hustle and flow.

The Five Circles

Imagine five concentric circles. These represent the people you know and interact with, and among whom you must choose your level of vulnerability.

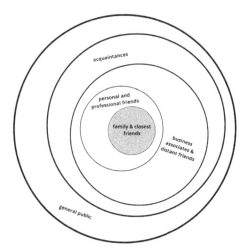

The inner circle includes your spouse, kids, some of your family, and closest friends. These are the people with whom you can share absolutely everything.

The second circle includes personal and professional friends, among whom you can share *most* everything.

The third circle of influence includes business associates and people with whom you're just getting friendly. More trouble occurs at this level than anywhere else. Lines get crossed here when you may be anxious to connect with others or "be authentic." It may be the case that you're with someone who can't hold space for your vulnerability or it simply isn't the time or place for it. Sometimes too much information is too much information.

The fourth and fifth circles are for acquaintances and strangers or the general public.

The ultimate goal is for you to have peace and balance between hustle and flow, receiving support from each circle in response to the level of vulnerability you're sharing with them.

You are certainly free to disclose over a few circles, and the internet is full of examples of people sharing the most intimate details of their lives on Facebook or LinkedIn. Again, if that's your authentic brand and the way that you approach life, that's wonderful. Be deliberate and proactive.

In addition to considering how transparency serves your goals, at all times you must be ready and responsible for the potential outcomes. Are you ready for any response to your personal share? Even if you intended to receive kindness, you may get rejected.

Recently, my daughter asked me what she should do about a situation in school. She overheard another classmate struggling with how to compose an essay. My daughter has a very disciplined approach, great notes on the format, and even developed an acronym to help her remember it. She wanted to share it with the classmate who's been having trouble, and asked me what I thought.

I told her it is a wonderful thing to have the impulse to reach out, to want to help someone else. *But was she prepared for any response from the other girl?* As much as we might wish otherwise, it is not the other person's responsibility to be kind. The classmate could love and gratefully accept what my daughter meaningfully had to contribute. But she also could tell her to buzz off and keep out of it. Was my daughter willing to accept the possibility of that outcome?

I am reminded of a great quote, again from Epictetus: "If anyone tells you that a certain person speaks ill of you, do not make excuses about what is said of you but answer, 'He was ignorant of my other faults, else he would not have mentioned these alone.'"

In all things, it pays to have a good sense of humor.

Prodro Pro Tip: Always be prepared for a variety of possible outcomes, especially when you're making a substantial risk—in finances, business, relationships, or emotions.

Meeting Your Human Potential

Personal excellence is the holy grail of achievement in my book: Continuously striving to bring a higher level of performance to any situation, conversation, work or school opportunity will get you results that make you happier and more abundant.

Confidence, self-concept, and self-esteem are major determinants here. There is a multifaceted, billion-dollar industry built around these concepts that can help you manage the delicate balance of how you were raised, what you've achieved, and your own particular psychological and emotional ecology.

For the sake of *this* conversation on personal excellence, however, let's level the playing field and assert that you have access to the universal human potential: *you can achieve anything*. People have achieved excellence against all odds. So, take the judgment out of it and suspend your beliefs about yourself at this particular point. There is no doubt you will look for evidence to support you either way, in the form of personal history (what you've tried, and where you succeeded or failed), or statistics (what other people have done in the past). But neither are useful metrics for assessing your potential, as they are each relative and based on the past—which certainly does not equal the future.

Your potential is not found in comparisons to anyone in your family, nor to those with the same income, social circle or peer group, experience, skill, or industry. None of these have anything to do with your inherent human potential.

Real magic happens when you decide and declare the level of excellence you're going for, and that you are going all in. You are going to increase your standards and are not going to settle for less.

You may also be completely happy with where you are. If that's the case, there are other useful questions:

- Is there more? (Yes!)
- How can I maintain what I've got?
- Should I expand the level of excellence I've already achieved into philanthropy or charitable endeavors?
- How can I continue to up-level my quality of life?
- How can I continue to serve in more impactful, meaningful ways?

Many people confuse activity with deliberate, determined action. Increasing excellence includes learning better, faster ways to accomplish goals

There is no upper limit, no finish line in this view of human potential. Stay open, curious, committed, and humble, and you'll discover ever more opportunities for the expression of your own unique human potential.

<u>Prodro Pro Tip</u>: Ask: What are the first three words I use to describe myself? Who are the five people that I spend the most time with? How do they impact my goals?

CHAPTER 9 GUIDED JOURNALING EXERCISE

1. **What are three things I think about over and over every day?**

    About your health:
    About your family:
    About your career:
    About your opportunities in life:

2. **What do I really want?**

    Relationship:
    Career:
    Finance:
    Health:
    Other:

3. **What would I do if I knew I could not fail?**

The Big Idea: What you focus on expands, good or bad. That is so profound. Let's embrace it again: *What you focus on expands.* Where your thoughts go, your energy flows. The greatest power you have as a human is to direct and choose your thoughts.

CHAPTER 10

THE SECOND QUESTION: WHO CAN I SERVE?

Wisdom isn't about accumulating more facts; it's about understanding big truths in a deeper way. -Melinda Gates, The Moment of Lift

Connect and Network

I was 14 years old when I first read Dale Carnegie's *How to Win Friends and Influence People*. I have always carried its timeless principles with me along with my heritage, my parents, and family. As a member of a huge Greek family with *extensive* communication skills and a widely-expressed zest for life, I had *no chance* to be quiet or not learn how to be heard. This was incredibly good fortune, because one of the most coveted business skills is connecting with prospective customers and staff to influence people. Thus, it is important to master the art of communication and conversation, to be able to find common ground and move with hustle and flow.

I find the term *networking* a little bit old and stale. The goal is making true connections. In this chapter, I want to talk about the balance of hustle and flow in forming new relationships with others. This comes very naturally to me after years of great failures and successes, so it is my most sincere hope that my life experience can serve you. This is what inspired me to write this book.

Prodro Pro Tip: When you attend a networking event, contribute as much as you gain. Consider every social opportunity a two-way street. When you enter a room, bring to mind what you can offer from meeting new people. You have a *lot* to offer even if you currently hold an entry level position. I always appreciate great questions, that is something you can add to a conversation or new connection.

Have insights. Take an interest in other people. Remember the point of any networking event is to create authentic, genuine connections with people that you can follow up with and with whom you can exchange ideas, thoughts, and time to be of genuine service to one another. There's no harm in having a goal and a plan for each event. People mistakenly believe that fluency at networking events is something you either have or you don't, and that conversation should be spontaneous and authentic. Yes, but it is also a good idea to pause before you go to review your current position, what you want to say, and what you are actively creating.

At different points in our lives, we look to accomplish different things. Our focus changes over time. There are probably 10 different ways you could describe where you are and what you are trying to accomplish at any particular event, so it helps to *craft* the lead sentences about yourself and your lead question for other people. These are two very simple, vital keys to make sure that you put forward a deliberate, thoughtful presence at each networking function.

First, let's consider your first statement or sentence about yourself. It is true that you can never get a second chance to make a first impression. The first thing out of your mouth is going to set the tone. How do you want to describe yourself? Often, people describe themselves by what they do, where they come from, how old they are, or what their current position is:

- "Hi, I'm Lisa and I'm an orthopedic nurse."

This tone is very direct. It says what her focus is, what she does and is very specific. You could also lead with something more general and open-ended and say:

- "I'm Lisa and I'm in healthcare. I focus on children's issues."
- "I'm Lisa. I'm a healthcare specialist looking for new ways to improve the lives of children."

Three examples, three different ways to approach the same thing. You decide how broadly you wish to cast your net. A more general or broad conversation will entertain a broader audience. If you're at a convention of nurses, of course you need specificity. But if you're at a Chamber of Commerce event or something that has a broad audience, giving a more general description and then saying at the end, "I'm a pediatric orthopedic nurse," will invite more meaningful conversation.

The 30-Second Sound-Bite Conversation

When you become an expert in this, you unlock a key to the great space between hustle and flow. This skill will reap rewards among colleagues, customers, and potential allies of all sorts. Here is how it works: Always have a goal in mind for the desired outcome of the conversation. For example, a supplier and a prospective customer run into each other at a networking event. What they talk about and how they approach the conversation will dictate the success of that interaction. There's something to be said for letting things flow naturally, but the best salespeople on earth—the best converters, influencers and leaders—make the most out of their sound bites.

Let's pretend you are the supplier in this example. You are at a networking event. You see your prospective customer approaching. Intentionally create balance and flow by asking a question to engage her. It is always best to start there, but you need to make a point, connect, and exit. The idea is to leave them wanting more—not feeling like their ears are bleeding.

The art comes in being able to manage the other person's response, because they might go on and on. You could lose your 30 second sound bite and with it, your opportunity to move to the next interaction. Remember that you have a goal in mind. Whether you want a phone appointment with them, to send them information, invite them to a golf outing, or land an introduction, bring the goal to mind very quickly when you see them.

Clarity and Precision

Relationship building should never be contrived. It is deliberate. It makes the most of someone's time and thereby shows them tremendous respect. If you are clear about what will move the relationship forward, good things happen. Let's imagine that you are approaching a new contact and you've decided your goal in this conversation is to get an appointment with them.

This is the gold standard in terms of goals because their willingness to meet again means that they see value in what you're doing.

Instead of asking, "How are you?" ask an open-ended question that has a creative twist and demonstrates that you've done up-to-date research. In this particular case, you found a press release on their website announcing they are currently launching a new diversity initiative. Even though the diversity initiative has nothing to do with your goal of setting an appointment, it's something to do with their company. I recommend always putting people at ease by building rapport or making a connection first. Asking straight out for a meeting would be too aggressive.

A bridge-building question could be, "Hey, Paul. It's great to see you. I see that on your website that your company is launching a diversity initiative. That is amazing. Does that affect your division?"

In this way, you establish rapport. Maybe it works, maybe it doesn't. Paul might say, "Yeah, they're making us attend this," or "No, it really doesn't have any effect on me. It's just a policy." Then you launch to the next point. How do you know what to say? Just pick something. It's not always going to be the right thing. You're not always going to have a big spark of connection. But it is still a great way to subtly communicate that you are well-versed in what's going on in their company. It puts you in a different position than a stranger who comes out asking for something.

It is possible you strike a nerve with your opener, and he starts gushing about all the details. Remember, however, that you have a goal and only 30 seconds before you've got to exit. You must get to the point.

There is a subtle art to elegantly redirecting a conversation. You've got to get to the other people; that's what you're there for. You can say, "Wow, that's intense, Paul. I see how it's really affecting your department. I'd love to learn more about that. Can you stay after the luncheon? I really want to have more time to hear what you're going through."

This way, you've honored what he's saying. You're not cutting him off abruptly by saying, "Wow, you know, that was really interesting, but I don't care." And you're showing the other person respect and asking for follow up time. He may say yes, and then you've met your goal. If he says "No, no, I'm just venting about that," you have a chance to pivot. You can say, "Well, I'd still like to schedule some time to reconnect with you. This is a really great conversation. Would you be available Tuesday at 9?"

In this way, you've achieved your original goal of asking for a meeting.

If you researched Paul and decided he would be a meaningful contact, then remember your *real goal* is not just an appointment, but to create a lasting connection. You're in it for the long game. The worst-case scenario is if Paul starts talking more about how the diversity initiative is affecting him and it seems unnatural to segue into setting the appointment. The great thing is that you're going to have a follow-up opportunity. You found something that matters to Paul!

The Most Interesting Person in the Room

Throughout my career, I have made a commitment and an investment in being the most interesting person in the room. It's not an ego trip, rather it is a strategy and a goal that allows me to connect with people quickly and in significant ways that create win-win scenarios for everyone.

The key to being interesting is simply cultivating a love of learning so that you stay open to new ideas and knowledge. Research and learn a little bit across a wide variety of subjects, especially those you are not well versed in: advanced science, mechanics, fishing. I like to have a broad range of interests because *it's not really about what I know. It's about how well I can ask questions.* Even with a cursory level of knowledge about a given topic, I can freely engage in a conversation with somebody, learning about their field without being intrusive. People love to talk about themselves and are generally most interested in people who are interested in *them.*

People naturally migrate to you when you take a chance, attend different seminars, and read different articles, subscribe to publications for industries that you're not in, open your mind and heart to the perspectives of other countries, other people, and *listen*. This way, you become reasonably well-versed in a number of topics, and the connections you make are authentic and built on common ground.

If there's someone I want to meet, I always do my research on them before business networking events. I check out their public profiles to see what I might be able to relate to: which school they attended, what charities they volunteer for, any key items that may create a launching point for a conversation.

The best way to be the most interesting person in the room is to take pride in your interests but instead of trying to tell everybody what you know, *find the common bond.*

This is the magic. Find the spark, the place where you and they have something in common. It's like a puzzle. Arrive at that place during the course of the conversation, and then become a follow-up expert. Once you have determined there is an authentic connection and you want to stay in touch, keep that individual on your radar. Develop a system of sending them relevant and interesting articles, events, or opportunities, so they know you're thinking about them. Just like your introduction, your continued outreach is personalized and authentic. Your presence adds value to their lives.

Doesn't that sound interesting?

Prodro Pro Tip: Find a role model of an incredibly accomplished, interesting person. For me one has been Mindy Grossman, CEO of WW. Whenever I get stuck in business, I ask myself…what would Mindy Grossman do? (true story!)

The Power of Better Questions

"Successful people ask better questions and as a result, get better answers."
~ Anthony Robbins

Connecting with people is a two-way street of giving and receiving. Thus, we could all benefit from learning to ask better questions. Too many people lead with what they want from the other person. It's limiting because it doesn't offer anything interesting or useful in exchange, as a *contribution.*

The worst way to proceed is to ask someone to "pick their brain." *People do not want their brain picked.* It's not a cute expression or a good intention;

it means you want to take their hard-won wisdom and expertise without offering anything in return. Nevertheless, as a seasoned professional, when somebody approaches me I'm always open for an interaction, even if they don't feel like an expert and are just hoping to gain insight.

The best way to approach somebody with tremendous expertise is to be honest, specific, and authentic about what you want to learn from them. Have an engaging question in mind plus sincere follow-up questions that convey your genuine interest. For example, if you meet a successful journalist, rather than telling them your goal of working for the Associated Press, start with questions that will be interesting *for them to talk to you about,* that give insight into their process and how they got where they are. Don't ask for shortcuts.

Don't ask, "How did you get to where you are?" This general question may be flattering but it also communicates that you have no clue. Look for a specific and interesting facet that you want to learn about. For example, "At your level of success, you have a lot of markets that you could choose to work in. Why did you choose St. Louis?" Or, "How do you interact with your editor when you have a disagreement?"

Asking probing questions will get them to actually *think* about something they genuinely want to share with you. Better questions show that you care.

If you don't have expertise to share with them, that's okay. You can always become the most interesting person in the room by asking fantastic questions. In addition, keep a handful of good follow up questions and a thoughtful general question in your back pocket. For example, "Do you have a success tip you would offer to somebody who is looking for their first job?" This kind of question prompts people to think as a seasoned professional. Hands down, the most fun I have at events is when I get an opportunity to connect with somebody who asks me great questions that get me thinking, and I feel like it's a two-way communication.

Do Your Research

Hustle and flow won't work unless you do your research. You need good information to make split second decisions about pushing forward into creation and hustle and when to lay back, let things happen and let it flow. In the information age, you have unprecedented access to data and background on prospective customers. Before a meeting, go to a customer's website and check out their press releases to get a feel for their company culture, their key issues, and what's going on for them at the moment. Review all of their social media profiles.

Next, I recommend that you research, develop, and follow your own personal Dream Team. Assemble your aspirational team of advisors, the board of directors of your dreams. They can be very, very high level—people whom you currently think you will never have the opportunity to meet in person. (Your chances will go up significantly if you identify, assemble, and pay attention to them!)

Some of the members of my Dream Team included Anthony Robbins, Oprah Winfrey, Peter Diamandis, and Deepak Chopra.

The purpose of this exercise is to brainstorm a high-level team of advisors and people who match your character and integrity. Frame it out: how is what they represent congruent with what you are trying to accomplish or achieve? Next, monitor their work. Notice what they are focusing on, speaking about, or writing. I create profiles of each member of my Dream Team. I print out their bio and headshots, and set a Google Alert for news about their work. I subscribe to their newsletters, blogs, and social channels.

By doing this, you are creating something from nothing. You are moving, as Dr. Dyer says, "from nowhere to now here." You have begun to call your Dream Team forward. Stay connected to the work of your dream advisory council. If you follow closely enough, it will feel as if they are talking directly to you.

Prior to attending an event, I profile the most important people I want to connect with, including the keynote speakers, the organizer, the sales and catering manager from the facility, and the house manager of the venue or convention center. If the mayor is going to attend, I may create a profile on him or her, highlighting one or two interesting and unique things they've been working on. During the event, if I'm afforded 30 seconds with any of these people, I know something about them. Plus, I've got something interesting and compelling to say.

You would be surprised how many people attend events and can't recognize the keynote speaker. If you're going to spend your time and energy at events with the prospect of making high level connections, why not practice the hustle and flow?

Prodro Pro Tip: Do the hustle and the research before you arrive at an event or conference. Then, when you get to the event, let it flow. You can seize any chance or opportunity because you exude confidence of having done your research. You know who the person is and you can take 15 seconds to stop, stick your hand out and say, "Hi, I'm Theo and I am so excited to be here. I'm looking forward to the presentation today." If they engage, you could have a 30 second conversation for which you are totally prepared.

Wrap It Up

One of the critical keys people miss in successful communication is *knowing when to leave*. In the balance between hustle and flow, *people often do not know when to disengage*. If you get an opportunity to meet somebody and the person shows some interest, you've got 15 to 30 seconds. If you engage well, ask to connect with them on LinkedIn, or send them a white paper. You can always say "I'll follow you on social." Then, actually follow them and connect. There is a chance they manage or review their social media channel and will remember you. It is worth a shot!

If you have tended to your mindset, your research, and the priorities of key people you'd like to meet at the event, then you're going to have a goal and feel confident about what you'll do when you meet them. Stick to the essentials and treat others' time with the utmost value and respect.

Finally, being intentional and deliberate comes with confidence that you have something interesting and compelling to say that creates value. No matter the status or expertise of the person you are meeting, remember you offer a unique perspective. Otherwise, they wouldn't be there. You can contribute valuable insights and ideas. Don't forget they're human too, so don't stress. Act deliberately, do your research, have something to say, and be prepared for any opportunity that presents itself.

CHAPTER 10 GUIDED JOURNALING EXERCISE

1. **What is really interesting about me?**

2. **How do I enjoy connecting with people?**

3. **How do I answer the question, "What do you do?"**

The Big Idea: You are not what you do. Your insatiable curiosity and desire to learn and expand brought you to this book, and are also rewiring your brain in new ways right now. The most interesting person in the room is most often the one asking the best questions.

CHAPTER 11

THE THIRD QUESTION: HOW WILL I ADOPT THIS NEW AWARENESS?

> *There are moments in life when everything changes. Sometimes these moments come out of nowhere, ambushing you. Sometimes they approach from a distance and arrive so slowly and expectedly that change is nothing to be surprised about.*
> *~Randi Zuckerberg, Dot Complicated: Untangling Our Wired Lives*

Emerging Opportunities

Emerging opportunities are ways for people to grow an already-launched business or expand an existing brand. Perhaps a new contact approached you or a new idea has caught your attention that would move you in a direction or a timeline you weren't planning. How do you know if it's a worthwhile change of course? And is there a formalized process for evaluating emerging opportunities?

I receive many questions about the best way to handle unexpected emerging opportunities, and here are my tried-and-true tips:

- First, does it *seem* too good to be true? If so, it probably is.

For example, if someone sells you hard on an opportunity to source a product from abroad at a fraction of the cost, which you can then label and market under your brand name—and they'll pay for it and do everything for you but it's very urgent and now you're receiving calls from them 20 times a day—don't do it. This is someone who wants to piggyback on your success or sell you something.

- The more urgent and aggressive someone is, the more concerned I am.

This is not to say there aren't urgent or emergent opportunities that make sense. The majority of successful product launches and extensions make strategic use of immediacy, and quick-decision fire sales by somebody coming to market may be a good move. Just do your due diligence and don't get carried away.

- Your most valuable asset and number one commodity is your time.

If you choose to pursue an emerging opportunity, ensure it requires only a certain percentage of your time, as opposed to dominating it and veering you off course from your original business plan.

Trade Shows & Virtual Conferences

In the digital age, people can connect globally and reach huge numbers of people at any time in a variety of different ways. Yet nothing takes the place of face to face interactions. I have had the great fortune of attending and representing companies at trade shows in multiple industries from the Fashion and Boutique show to the International Beauty Show, to the Vision Expo and more.

The microcosm represented at trade shows represents the full business cycle. It starts with identifying your target market somewhere in the balance between hustle and flow. Hustle out with a business idea to find the one show in the one place with the greatest number of your target market. Once you locate a possibility, analyze whether it makes financial sense to reach these potential customers all at once.

If you're going to exhibit, you may have the opportunity prior to the show to generate buzz, interest, and participation. I recommend you participate in these special promotions. Focus on building pre-show excitement and build-up of who you are, what you do, and why attendees should come by and visit you in person.

When you actually attend the show, think about:

- Your physical booth
- What will set you apart
- What messages you have
- What point of sale you plan to offer
- How you can catch the attention and get the right audience within the trade organization to stop and engage with you.
- How to engage onsite customers and keep them engaged
- Who will represent your brand or company

Too many business owners miss the boat on sending the right people to represent them. Trade shows are one of the greatest training grounds out there, so some of your green salespeople absolutely must attend. Nothing can take the place of real-world experience of being put on the spot time and time again while effectively communicating with strangers and staying focused. Reiterating the presentation over and over again in different scenarios with different customers is a great experience. The sheer volume of it serves a training purpose and being face to face with customers brings your brand to life in a way that no other experience can provide.

Trade Show Communication

When people come up to your booth, engage them with a question. If you're in the middle of a conversation or your pitch and somebody else walks up, you have to either include them or ask them to wait a minute without losing their attention. This requires serious skills in multitasking, communication, and audience engagement. It is easy to take these interpersonal skills for granted but in a trade show environment the strengths and weaknesses become immediately apparent.

You need a point of engagement and a plan of how to qualify customers so you don't waste your time or theirs. I have seen too many fantastic presentations done for people who absolutely are *not the right target market* and instead just somebody who would listen.

Make sure your process is in place. Once you have them in the booth and you've gotten to engage with them, learn a little bit more and pique their interest. Maybe demonstrate the product. Make sure you have a clear-cut set of next steps that *you want them to take* because everybody's going to say that they're just gathering information.

"Okay, can I have a brochure and then move on?" You've lost that opportunity.

The more granular you can get and the more information you can gather on each potential lead, the better. Quantity of leads is much less important than quality, because you could just buy a database and reach the same end. With a few simple questions you can determine critical information from new leads.

This is where you're really going to be able to build a relationship and determine if they're potential long-term customers. After the show is over, making sure that your communication strategy with these customers is expedient and authentic but mindful that people will be bombarded with email immediately upon their return. Send an initial email if their decision must happen quickly, so you don't miss out. Otherwise, give new contacts a little time and then send a personalized email follow-up or make a phone call to determine or establish their level of interest and their timeline. Fill your sales pipeline. Virtual Conferences require the same personal communication skills. Be sure to master technology to maximize an effective online presence.

Prodro Pro Tip: Take detailed notes after interactions with customers. The biggest lost opportunity at trade shows is having volumes of people come into the booth and collecting their data, but keeping them as cold leads because you haven't written any notes about who they are or what they might be interested in. You only know that they stopped by. Now you have to start the conversation over again, long distance and long after their interest piqued. You don't have visuals or your charming personality to persuade them to make time for you. So booking follow-up appointments *at the trade show* is critical for people who have a high level of interest.

More Trade Show Hustle Tips

Be sure to walk the floor. There's no better way to shop your competition than to attend a trade show. Instead of searching on the internet, walk the floor and see their booths, talk to them, make friends with them. There's nothing wrong with friendly competition, having them know who you are. Just get a feel for what their brand is, or how they've engaged with customers, and you'll really get a grip on what you could do better.

You can start small with a regional show within your industry and build up from there. Tables at those smaller events can be wonderful, though they tend to have a more general audience. I don't see a tremendous value in events like those of the Chamber of Commerce, where people say that they're going there "to get their name out." Unless your target audience is a general audience, industry trade shows targeted toward your demographic is a better use of your time and money.

Take time to research the right trade shows. Try small regional ones and national industry shows so you can, again, see all of your competition. Consider cross-selling into a different market, into other industries' trade shows so that you stand out as the only one in that category.

Finally, research other vendors before committing to the trade show space and booth. Costs can be exorbitant but they potentially offer everything you need: pre-show marketing, onsite market marketing, sales training, engagement strategy, product demonstration, follow-up, special event marketing. Nothing can take the place of trade shows in bringing your brand to life.

Let the Naysayers Fuel You

I am a successful Amazon seller, but that wasn't always the case. Several years ago, a friend of my brother's who was doing very well on the platform told me it wouldn't be my thing because it had nothing to do with forming relationships. It was a big, huge company, I'd never meet anyone. In other words, my extroversion and my winning personality (LOL) wouldn't help me with Amazon. My skills did not apply there.

We'll see about that, I thought.

I got to *work*. I read everything they had. I did all of their training.

What I saw was that Amazon had all the customers, a lending program, as well as great marketing programs for advertising and for customer insights - in other words, everything was there to build up small businesses. They invited me to a Women's Entrepreneurship conference in Seattle. Again, this kid, a friend of my brother's, said "You're never gonna meet anybody there."

Cut to a few short months later. I was in Seattle to attend the conference. I did what I usually do and carefully researched all of the keynote speakers ahead of time. I also showed up to the event very early, before any other attendees arrived. I found myself in a hallway with a gentleman who looked familiar. It was one of the speakers! One of Jeff Bezos' key executives, in fact. I introduced myself and kept it very brief, saying only that I was Theo from Tampa and that I was thrilled to be there. I think I also may have mentioned how grateful I was for all of Amazon's awesome promotion tools for sellers like myself.

It was hustle, yet it was also flow, because I didn't cling or try to force a long conversation. A lot of people do this: when they see an opening or an opportunity, they launch into a huge elevator pitch and ruin a human moment. I didn't do that. I kept it short and simple.

And what do you know? The speaker got up on stage that morning and said, to a room full of thousands of people, "I just got to meet Theo from Tampa!"

It was amazing. And it was all thanks to me being who I am—living in the balance of hustle and flow.

CHAPTER 11 GUIDED JOURNALING EXERCISE

1. **An emerging opportunity for me is:**

2. **Trade shows remind me to show up as:**

3. **I would like to hustle and create:**

Big Idea: The one great equalizer in life, for all people, is time. No matter how tall or short, rich or poor, we all have the same number of hours in the day. A trade show is an opportunity for getting together with the like-minded people in one place, and to present your best self. Time is precious, use it wisely.

Conclusion: Living in a Different World

I began this book by telling you the story of the time I *didn't* meet the Dalai Lama. Finding out I could not travel to India—that I had spent thousands of dollars on tickets I would not be able to use—was extremely disappointing.

Some of my travel documents had my maiden name; some had my prior married name. I should have anticipated the issue, but then again, the powers that be *could* have used their discretion to let me fly. It doesn't ultimately matter. Choosing to live in the balance of hustle and flow is a never-ending intention to see the gifts in your situation no matter what is going on. Yes, it is much easier when things are going your way. But perhaps the decision means even more when they are not.

It looks like I'll have the opportunity to remember this lesson again very soon, because as I write this conclusion, the world is suffering from the novel coronavirus COVID-19 outbreak. It is particularly acute in Italy, where my family is all scheduled to vacation in two short months. I'm not sure how that story will end, or if we'll get to go, but I do know that no matter what happens, I will meet the people I need to meet and learn the lessons I need to learn.

What motivated me to write this book is my belief that it is *the decisions that we make on a daily basis* that reveal who we really are. We can behave with grace no matter what's going on.

I wish I could give you one standard rule for hustle and flow, but it's not that simple. Knowing when to hustle and when to flow is a very personal thing. I can't tell you when to do either one. You need to develop your own intuition and then honor it.

Develop your own criteria that you can apply to different scenarios. Consider your own risk tolerance, whether it's in your professional life or your personal life. As I get bolder, my risk tolerance is higher. I am willing to make mistakes, to try things, even to fail, because I have years of hustling behind me.

But that doesn't mean that I'm *only* hustle. I've learned to listen to cues in my life. To take a breather, to listen to my gut feeling, to give people space. To pay attention to how those in my social circle influence my decisions.

Sometimes the best things that happen in our lives occur at the intersection of hustle and flow. For example, I recently wrote a very personal article for International Women's Day. I'm a very positive, upbeat person. But this particular piece was a little bit edgier. It was about what happens in the workplace for women and how we can help each other when small micro-aggressions occur.

In the piece, I said we need to call these small moments out right away instead of letting them slide or discounting the experience of the woman. I called it the Immediate Response Challenge and I published on Thrive Global, which is Arianna Huffington's platform. I believe we can all build each other up and change the world by not allowing the small things to happen; by not discounting them and dismissing them. I cited an example and I tagged three of my favorite female leaders, Mindy Grossman, Melinda Gates, and Lori Grenier.

Mindy Grossman actually tweeted out the link to my article! I was delighted to have the CEO of a major company like Weight Watchers share my work.

I did hustle to make this happen. But I had to flow. I had to trust my instinct and write a piece that felt a little risky. It challenged all women to call out sexist or disrespectful workplace behaviors in the moment that are not okay, even when they are small things that usually get glossed over.

I would have never asked Mindy directly to share my piece. But it happened. That's flow.

What Will You Do Now?

As I said in the introduction to this book, an entirely different world is being created around us as we navigate the novel coronavirus COVID-19 pandemic. Families are staying home and figuring out new ways to work, play, learn, and live.

There is a positive side to all of it (yes, there is always a positive side) to spending more time at home and jumping out of the chaos of work, commuting, extracurricular activities, and (sadly) even work for some. It lies in the opportunity to ask yourself, "What will I do now?"

The Balance Between Hustle & Flow

This is a hustle question, but you can ask it in an intentional, deliberate way.

"How will I control what I can, and accept that which I cannot control?"

This is an opportunity for unprecedented reflection and growth. The time we spend quietly contemplating our next steps and approach to life can set us on a new and better course, set us free to pursue our higher goals and aspirations, and deepen your connections to others.

The option to do what you have always done is off the table. Through no fault of your own, you no longer have the status quo as an option. Critical providers like doctors, nurses, and other healthcare workers don't even get to stay the same. They have important decisions to make about working longer hours in potentially hazardous environments. They have to make a choice whether to continue working if it puts their families at risk, when every precaution in the world cannot guarantee their safety. We all benefit from the fact that most healthcare providers serve with a higher purpose and will continue to go to work despite the risks.

This awareness sets the stage for our own answer to the question, "What will I do now?" You have options. We are all fortunate to have personal options.

Being at home and creating new rituals and routines offers the opportunity to build the life you desire from scratch. Some of the limitations that existed because of time away from home are suspended. Will you begin a side project you have put off? Will you learn a new language, teach your children to cook, or even write a book?

Now is all we ever have. The present moment can bring you a convergence of your passion, purpose, connection, and goals aligned with your integrity. For me, I committed to completing this very book, as well as launching an online course and VIP Coaching program.

My deepest desire is to support you and enjoy the journey together.

Who Are You?

Our self-image and the answer to this question is usually answered by a description of what you do or your vocation, but I'd like you to go deeper here and answer this question in flow. Dr. Wayne once said, "You are not what you do, because if you are…then when you don't do that, you aren't." In a way, he was separating the self-identity of who you *are* from what you *do*.

That is step one. We rely on language to convey the details of who we are. Let's begin with the three words you use to describe yourself. Social media channel Twitter asks for three labels under your name. They give people a quick insight into who you are (or at least your version of it) so they can decide to follow or engage with you. Chances are good that you underestimate the power you have in describing yourself. Not to suggest that our social media profiles are the ultimate answer to this question, but rather, they can offer some clues on the journey to self-discovery.

Now is the time for a self-assessment of your core values and how they are being expressed in the world. Is how you are showing up in the world a true reflection of your integrity and what you value most? Are you working on and within your calling or passion? Take a quick inventory of the following topics and jot down who you are in these roles and topics.

Family: Child, Parent, Cousin, Sibling, Partner

Friends: Best Friend, Friend as close as family, Acquaintance

Work Colleague: Worker, Professional, Colleague, Influencer, Manager, Researcher, Service Provider

Global Citizen: Family, Friends, Work

Entrepreneur: Owner, Solopreneur, Inventor

Rate yourself on a scale of 1-10 on how closely you align with your purpose and integrity for each category. For example:

Family: Parent (9) I homeschool my 3 teenagers but there is always room for improvement!

Family: Child (10) My parents are not on Earth, but I honor by serving others and mention them often.

Entrepreneur/Owner: (9) I own several sustainable consumer brands and treat my employees with love and respect.

These are just a few real examples of my self-assessment. It will help you put words and numbers to who you are and how you spend your precious time on Earth. What are the three words you use to describe who you are? How can you make this time most valuable to align who you are with what you do?

My Challenge and Offering

I am passionate about living in the balance between hustle and flow because it is an inspiring place to be. For additional guidance on how to achieve balance in your own life, I invite you to go deeper into this work with me. Visit connectwiththeo.com for additional free resources.

Light your fire!

I look forward to seeing you there.

Conclusion Guided Journaling Exercise

1. **What I discovered about myself:**

2. **My next steps are:**

3. **I can't wait to:**

4. **I can improve on:**

5. **The most curious incidents, signs, and roadblocks I have encountered in the last few years are:**

I have approached them with the following mindset/ actions:

Hustle (i.e., I decided to reschedule my party till after the stay at home order and did a zoom party in the meantime.)

Flow (i.e., I forgave my sister-in-law for telling my boss something that got me fired.)

6. **I am most grateful for:**

REFERENCES

Angelou, Maya. "My mission in life…" https://www.goodreads.com/quotes/11877-my-mission-in-life-is-not-merely-to-survive-but Accessed March 27, 2020.

Burton, Dr. Neel. "Jung: The Man and His Symbols," https://www.psychologytoday.com/us/blog/hide-and-seek/201204/jung-the-man-and-his-symbols Accessed March 27, 2020.

Dyer, Dr. Wayne. "Success Secrets," https://www.drwaynedyer.com/blog/success-secrets/ Accessed March 15, 2020.

Dyer, Dr. Wayne. *"Real Magic: Creating Miracles in Everyday Life",* p.9, Harper Collins, New York: 2010.

Gates, Melinda. *The Moment of Lift,* Flat Iron Books, New York, NY. 2019.

"Honoring Martin Luther King Jr: Life's Most Persistent and Urgent Question," https://blog.mass.gov/hhs/uncategorized/honoring-martin-luther-king-jr-lifes-most-persistent-and-urgent-question/ Accessed March 27, 2020.

"I will never attend an anti-war…" https://www.goodreads.com/quotes/859052-i-will-never-attend-an-anti-war-rally-if-you-have Accessed March 27, 2020.

Maraboli, Steve. *Life, the Truth, and Being Free,* A Better Today Publishing, 2009.

Moore, James T. *"One and Only You,"* https://www.symphonyoflove.net/blog/139/one-and-only-you.html Accessed March 27, 2020.

Noël, Reginald A. "Race, Economics, And Social Status," https://www.bls.gov/spotlight/2018/race-economics-and-social-status/pdf/race-economics-and-social-status.pdf Accessed March 15, 2020.

Panagiotakos, Demosthenes, et. al. "Sociodemographic and Lifestyle Statistics of Oldest Old People (>80 Years) Living in Ikaria Island: The Ikaria Study," Cardiol Res Pract. https://www.ncbi.nlm.nih.gov/pmc/articles/PMC3051199/ 2011.

Pattakos, Alex & Dundon, Elaine. *The OPA Way: Finding Joy & Meaning in Everyday Life & Work.* BenBella Books, 2014.

Robbins, Tony. "How to Make a Massive Action Plan," https://www.tonyrobbins.com/career-business/how-to-make-a-massive-action-plan-map/ Accessed March 27, 2020.

Robbins, Tony. "Ask Better Questions," https://www.tonyrobbins.com/mind-meaning/ask-better-questions/ Accessed March 27, 2020.

Rohn, Jim. "You're the average..." https://www.businessinsider.com/jim-rohn-youre-the-average-of-the-five-people-you-spend-the-most-time-with-2012-7 Accessed March 27, 2020.

Roosevelt, Theodore. "Citizenship is a Republic Speech," https://www.leadershipnow.com/leadingblog/2010/04/theodore_roosevelts_the_man_in.html Accessed March 15, 2020.

Twain, Mark. "Forgiveness is the fragrance..." https://www.goodreads.com/quotes/1708-forgiveness-is-the-fragrance-that-the-violet-sheds-on-the Accessed March 27, 2020.

Welch, Jack. "As a Leader, You Must Give Yourself This Mirror Test," https://jackwelch.strayer.edu/winning/mirror-test-leader/ Accessed March 27, 2020.

"What is EMDR?" https://www.emdr.com/what-is-emdr/ Accessed March 27, 2020.

Zuckerberg, Randi. "How to Live Your Life, Guilt-Free," https://www.marieclaire.com/career-advice/a20722543/randi-zuckerberg-pick-three/ Accessed March 27, 2020.

Zuckerberg, Randi. *Dot Complicated: Untangling Our Wired Lives,* Harper Collins, New York, NY. 2013.

Zukov, Gary. *Seat of the Soul,* Simon & Schuster, New York, NY. 1989.

VIDEO RESOURCES

Flow

Dr. Wayne Dyer - 'I AM THAT I AM' - Powerful Meditation
Manifesting Your Soul's Purpose with Dr. Wayne Dyer

Staying Conscious in the Face of Adversity | A Special Message From Eckhart Tolle
Rewired with Dr. Joe Dispenza | Gaia
5 Steps to Change Your Life with Dr. Joe Dispenza

Put God First - Denzel Washington Motivational & Inspiring Commencement Speech
Soul to Soul with Dr. Maya Angelou, Part 1 | SuperSoul Sunday | Oprah Winfrey Network

Hustle

Tony Robbins' TED Talk
Tony Robbins' Secret to Energy for Life
It's Not OVER Until You Win! Your Dream is Possible - Les Brown
Will Smith's Life Advice Will Change You - One of the Greatest Speeches Ever | Will Smith Motivation

Balance Between Hustle and Flow

Oprah on Believing in Yourself | Oprah's Lifeclass | Oprah Winfrey Network
Gary Zukav: The New Perception of Community with Oprah Winfrey | SuperSoul Sessions | OWN
The power of vulnerability | Brené Brown
Listening to shame | Brené Brown

ADDITIONAL RESOURCES: BOOKS

The Bible
How to Win Friends and Influence People by Dale Carnegie
Psycho Cybernetics by Dr. Maxwell Maltz
The Urantia Book by Anonymous
Anatomy of an Illness by Norman Cousins
Think and Grow Rich by Napoleon Hill
Unlimited Power by Tony Robbins
Real Magic and Your Sacred Self by Dr. Wayne Dyer (every single one of his books)
Man's Search for Meaning by Viktor Frankl
See You At the Top by Zig Ziglar
Seat of the Soul by Gary Zukav
Silver Boxes by Florence Littauer
The Hero's Journey by Joseph Campbell
The 100 Greatest Ideas of All Time by The Teaching Company
The Secret by Rhonda Byrne
The Four Agreements by Miguel Ruiz
The Success Principles by Jack Canfield
The Innovators by Walter Iaasacson
Einstein by Walter Iaasacson
Zero to One by Peter Thiel
Daring Greatly by Brene Brown
Pick Three by Randi Zuckerberg

ABOUT THE AUTHOR

Theo Prodromitis is an award-winning entrepreneur, Amazon Seller, marketing strategist, philanthropist and Greek mom. She is the CEO and co-founder of Spa Destinations and CEO of Out Front Brands. Her passion for business is grounded in her love of "*philotimo,*" the Greek cultural imperative to serve the greater good with honor. Theo is a best-selling author of *The Success Formula* together with Jack Canfield and *Big Questions for Tough Times.*

A fierce advocate for women and small businesses, she is a United States House of Representatives Small Business Committee Congressional Witness and serves on the National Retail Federation Retail Advisory Council. Her awards include NRF Champion of Retail and 2020 Enterprising Women of the Year. Theo was the Executive Producer of the documentary "Dreamer" with 11-time Emmy Award winning Director Nick Nanton about the world's most innovative entrepreneurs. Theo is also a founding member of the Zuckerberg Institute, Randi Zuckerberg's initiative to empower worldwide entrepreneurship and women in STEM.

Theo was featured in National Retail Federation's Retail Gets Real, Small Business Journal on International Women's Day, Business News Daily, Tampa Bay Times and Small Biz Daily. Amazon features include: Amazon Blog, Day One, Stories of Entrepreneurship, Storefront Women-Owned Business feature and Storefront of the Week, Yahoo Finance, Bay News 9, ABC Action News, FOX 13 and NBC and the Money section of USA Today.

Theo earned a Bachelor's degree in Political Science from the University of South Florida and a Yale University Certificate in The Science of Well Being. She is the dedicated mother of Mary, Jacqueline and Spero and the intrepid organizer of her big Greek family reunions.

CPSIA information can be obtained
at www.ICGtesting.com
Printed in the USA
LVHW040946161020
668887LV00006B/335

9 781982 253653